MW01055014

MAKE-AHEAD
BABY FOOD
COOKBOOK

MAKE-AHEAD BABY FOOD COOKBOOK

STEPHANIE VAN'T ZELFDEN, RDN, CDN

Photography by Nadine Greeff

ROCKRIDGE PRESS

Copyright © 2020 by Rockridge Press, Emeryville, California

No part of this publication may be reproduced, stored in a retrieval system, or transmitted in any form or by any means, electronic, mechanical, photocopying, recording, scanning, or otherwise, except as permitted under Sections 107 or 108 of the 1976 United States Copyright Act, without the prior written permission of the Publisher. Requests to the Publisher for permission should be addressed to the Permissions Department, Rockridge Press, 6005 Shellmound Street, Suite 175, Emeryville, CA 94608.

Limit of Liability/Disclaimer of Warranty: The Publisher and the author make no representations or warranties with respect to the accuracy or completeness of the contents of this work and specifically disclaim all warranties, including without limitation warranties of fitness for a particular purpose. No warranty may be created or extended by sales or promotional materials. The advice and strategies contained herein may not be suitable for every situation. This work is sold with the understanding that the Publisher is not engaged in rendering medical, legal, or other professional advice or services. If professional assistance is required, the services of a competent professional person should be sought. Neither the Publisher nor the author shall be liable for damages arising herefrom. The fact that an individual, organization, or website is referred to in this work as a citation and/or potential source of further information does not mean that the author or the Publisher endorses the information the individual, organization, or website may provide or recommendations they/it may make. Further, readers should be aware that websites listed in this work may have changed or disappeared between when this work was written and when it is read.

For general information on our other products and services or to obtain technical support, please contact our Customer Care Department within the United States at (866) 744-2665, or outside the United States at (510) 253-0500.

Rockridge Press publishes its books in a variety of electronic and print formats. Some content that appears in print may not be available in electronic books, and vice versa.

TRADEMARKS: Rockridge Press and the Rockridge Press logo are trademarks or registered trademarks of Callisto Media Inc. and/or its affiliates, in the United States and other countries, and may not be used without written permission. All other trademarks are the property of their respective owners. Rockridge Press is not associated with any product or vendor mentioned in this book.

Interior and Cover Designer: Lindsey Dekker
Art Producer: Megan Baggott
Editor: Kayla Park
Production Editor: Mia Moran
Photography © 2020 Nadine Greeff
Author photo courtesy of Eric Van't Zelfden
ISBN: Print 978-1-64611-909-7 | eBook 978-1-64611-910-3
R0

For Ava, my sunshine

CONTENTS

GREEN PEA PURÉE, PAGE 43; VERY BERRY SMOOTHIE, PAGE 73; PEANUT BUTTER PURÉE, PAGE 56; MANGO PURÉE, PAGE 42; BLUEBERRY PURÉE, PAGE 41; BLACK BEAN PURÉE, PAGE 52

INTRODUCTION

I was so excited to introduce my daughter, Ava, to solid foods. I was even more excited to cook for her.

I knew her first food would be my favorite: avocado. Next, I really wanted her to try applesauce, oatmeal, sweet potatoes, and green peas. Past that, I figured, I could just wing it, right?

Nope. Turns out that little babies have big bellies. I was prepared for the first few weeks of food, but once she started eating multiple meals a day, I struggled to keep up. It was time for a new plan.

I sat down and mapped out all the different foods and nutrients I wanted to introduce to Ava. Fruits and vegetables like mangos, peaches, carrots, and spinach. Iron-rich foods like eggs and lentils. Bold flavors like cinnamon, garlic, and lemon. I went grocery shopping, dug out the extra ice cube trays from the back of the cabinet, and cleared a shelf in the freezer. One afternoon, Ava went on an adventure with Daddy while I steamed, puréed, and froze enough foods to last her a month. After that, we were on our way.

Making homemade baby food may seem like a daunting task, but with a solid plan, I promise you it doesn't have to be. It will take some time and effort, but with the process outlined in this book, it'll be quicker and easier than you'd expect, and you can make baby food on your schedule to freeze for later. With your freezer stocked, preparing your baby's next meal is just as simple as opening a jar of store-bought baby food, but way tastier.

This book has everything you need to get started. It combines my professional guidance as a registered dietitian nutritionist with my personal experiences as a mom. First, you'll learn about the benefits of homemade baby food, and how to introduce foods in stages to help your baby transition to table foods smoothly. Then, you'll find all the tools and tips you need to make your baby food ahead of time, safely and efficiently. And within each chapter of baby food recipes, you'll find a four-week-long nutritionally balanced meal plan and shopping list—your complete guide for the month. Once the month flies by (and it will!), either repeat the meal plan or adapt it, including your family's favorite ingredients and flavors.

I'm so excited for you to embark on this journey to homemade delicious, nutritious baby food. By making your own baby food, you're giving your baby the best start possible, feeding them all the nutrients they need to grow and thrive, and creating wonderful memories together in the kitchen.

PART I

A MAKE-AHEAD BABY FOOD PRIMER

BUTTERNUT SQUASH AND LENTIL STEW, PAGE 85

You're at the supermarket, browsing the baby food aisle, staring at all those tiny jars. You look at them and think, "What's in these anyway?" and "How long have they been on the shelf?" and "Two dollars?! For one little jar?"

You're asking the right questions. The fact is, prepackaged baby food is a convenience. It's great if you're in a bind, but it's not healthier, tastier, or safer than homemade baby food.

Homemade baby food is one of the best gifts you can give your baby. It's fresh, nutritious, and affordable. And it's easier to make than you think. You can prepare it ahead of time and on your schedule, so even as a working parent, you don't have to rely solely on jars and pouches.

In this chapter, you'll learn how homemade baby food can benefit your baby, how to determine if your baby is ready for solid foods, and how to start serving solid foods.

BENEFITS OF FRESH OVER PREPACKAGED BABY FOOD

When you make your own baby food, you're giving your baby the freshest ingredients and the brightest flavors, and you're creating lasting family memories. As your baby gets older, cooking and sharing meals together will help them meet all their nutritional needs and develop healthy eating habits that will stick with them long into adulthood. Making your own baby food can also lead to healthier habits for the rest of the family, because home cooking is almost always healthier than packaged food or takeout.

Here are just a few of the benefits to making homemade baby food.

NUTRITION ADVANTAGE

Like all canned or jarred foods, prepackaged baby foods are pasteurized. Pasteurization makes a food shelf-stable by heating it to a very high temperature, but that heat can also remove some of the vitamins. Because of processing, prepackaged baby food may contain fewer nutrients than homemade baby food.

Prepackaged baby food is almost always low in fat. And babies *do not* need to be on a low-fat diet. Babies need about 50 percent of their daily calories to come from fat, which helps them absorb vitamins A, D, E, and K and gives them energy for all that growing they're doing!

COST SAVINGS

There's a lot that goes into prepackaged baby food besides just the food. When you purchase baby food, you're also paying for the tiny little jars, the cute labels, the research and development, and the marketing expenses. But when you make your own baby food, all you're paying for is the food. A typical 4-ounce jar or tub of sweet potato baby food can cost you $1 to $1.50. Instead, you can buy a pound of fresh sweet potatoes for the same price and get 20 ounces of homemade sweet potato baby food. It's the same price, but you get five times more food!

BETTER QUALITY CONTROL

When you make your own baby food, you're the one deciding what goes into it. You get to pick exactly which carrots, apples, and lentils to use. Food companies often add lemon juice or ascorbic acid (vitamin C) as a preservative, but this tends to make the food taste a little sour. They also like to add fruit juice concentrates for sweetness and to replace some of the flavor lost during processing, but this makes everything taste the same. With your homemade food, you won't need lemon juice or concentrated apple juice. Your food will taste bright and fresh all on its own.

RAISING A FOOD-FRIENDLY EATER

One of the best reasons to make your own baby food is you can customize it with your favorite spices, seasonings, and unexpected flavor combinations (think: peaches and peas—it could work!). This keeps your baby's taste buds intrigued and excited and helps your child become a more adventurous eater.

Homemade baby food also helps your baby transition through textures more easily. Babies don't transition from Stage 1 to Stage 2 overnight. It happens gradually, as babies learn to chew and tolerate different textures. With homemade baby food, you can customize the texture to match your baby's stage of development.

SIGNS YOUR BABY IS READY FOR SOLID FOODS

Each baby is unique, so you'll want to watch for specific signs that your baby is ready to get in that highchair and start eating.

On average, babies are ready for solid foods at around six months old. Some may be ready a little earlier, some a little later. Pediatricians recommend you don't start giving solid foods before four months old because your baby's digestive system isn't mature enough and introducing solid foods too early can increase their risk for infection as well as for developing food allergies.

HOW TO FINESSE A PICKY EATER

Try not to take it personally if your baby doesn't give your cooking a five-star review! Remember, this is all new to them. It can take at least 10 exposures before your baby will accept a new food. Don't give up; it takes time!

At around one to two years old, it's very common to see "picky eating" behaviors emerge. Your toddler might shun new foods, only ask for specific items, or suddenly dislike flavors they previously loved. Don't stress. This phase is normal, and most kids outgrow it by four to five years old.

Try these tips to create a calm, positive mealtime environment that helps even the pickiest eater try new foods:

- Lead by example. If you want your child to eat a food, show them how much you love it.

- Let your child feed themselves and play with their food. Embrace the mess!

- Give small portions of new food—like a single pea. Too much can be overwhelming.

- Give a choice between two options. Carrots or peas? Apples or bananas?

- Keep mealtime pressure-free. If your child refuses a food, you can say, "That's okay, you don't have to eat it." Once that pressure is off, they might just choose it on their own.

- Don't use food as a bribe. "If you eat your broccoli, you can have a cookie" might make them take a bite of broccoli today, but it won't help them like it tomorrow.

Some signs your baby is ready for solid foods include:

Good head control. Your baby should be able to hold their head up well and for an extended period.

Ability to sit up with support. Your baby doesn't need to be a total pro at sitting, but they should be able to sit up with only a little support.

Loss of tongue thrust. When babies are born, their tongues naturally push things out of their mouth. Around six months, that movement starts to fade, allowing them to swallow food.

Opens mouth to accept food. Your baby should show an interest in food and open their mouth to accept a spoon. Lots of babies do this anyway (because, *Hey, what's that stuff Dada's got? That looks fun!*), so be sure they are showing the other signs as well.

Never hesitate to ask your pediatrician for advice about starting solid foods. They can help address any specific questions or concerns you have.

FEEDING TIMELINE AND GUIDELINES

When you're first starting to give your baby solid foods, it feels like the changes are never-ending. While true, this is actually a good thing. Your baby won't be eating puréed foods for very long. The goal is to help your baby transition from purées to family food and learn to feed themselves within a few months.

This section will describe how this transition from puréed food to family food happens, including acclimating to the changes in textures, creating a feeding schedule, and prioritizing foods based on their nutrients. You'll also learn best practices for mealtime to make it a safe and relaxed experience.

ORDER OF SOLID FOOD INTRODUCTION

Baby food is divided into three stages, as described below. As your baby learns how to chew and swallow solid foods, they advance through the stages to experience more complex and challenging textures.

There's no need to start foods in a particular order. Years ago, rice cereal was the go-to first food. But we now know you can start with almost any food. Dietitians will tell you that as long as it's a safe texture, baby's first food can be almost anything, including avocado, eggs, beef, yogurt, tomato, strawberry, chicken, and broccoli.

Stage 1 Puréed: Around 6 months old, many babies are ready to start eating solid foods. These first foods are smooth and runny, to help your baby get used to eating new foods. New foods should be introduced one at a time, every two to three days, so if your baby has a reaction, it's easy to pinpoint what caused it. After your baby eats a food several times with no reaction, you can start combining foods for more variety.

Stage 2 Chunky: Once your baby has gotten the hang of purées and can easily bring food to the back of their mouth and swallow, around seven or eight months, you can introduce thicker and chunkier textures. This lets your baby practice chewing, which brings them one step closer to eating the same foods as the rest of the family.

Stage 3 Finger Foods: Around nine months, your baby is working on their pincer grasp, where they pick up small objects between their thumb and forefinger. What better way to practice than with finger foods! Stage 3 foods are soft and easy to chew, but served in small pieces so your baby can perfect that pincer grasp and practice chewing firmer textures.

NUTRIENTS TO PRIORITIZE

When planning your baby's meals, include foods that are rich in these four nutrients. These are especially important for your baby's growth, although they can be a bit more challenging to incorporate into their diet without a little planning.

Iron: Iron deficiency is one of the most common infant and childhood nutrient deficiencies. Iron is necessary for growth and the development of red blood cells, which carry oxygen throughout the body. Too little iron can lead to anemia, irritability, poor appetite, and lethargy. Plan to serve your baby two iron-rich foods each day, including meat, poultry, beans, lentils, eggs, and fortified cereals.

Fat: Fat makes up nearly half of an infant's daily calorie needs. It's the fuel for rapid growth, helps them absorb vitamins A, D, E, and K, and supports healthy brain development. Plan to serve one high-fat food with each meal, such as full-fat yogurt, avocado, olive oil, butter, peanut butter, other nut butters, meat, or fatty fish.

Omega-3 fatty acids: Omega-3 fatty acids support eye and brain development. There aren't many natural sources of omega-3 fatty acids, but you can serve fish (salmon, sardines, light tuna), flaxseeds, chia seeds, and omega-3–fortified eggs and milk. Plan to serve an omega-3–rich food two to three times each week.

Vitamin D: Vitamin D helps with proper bone development. While your baby can get some vitamin D from being out in the sun, many pediatricians recommend a supplement. In addition, serve your baby foods high in vitamin D, including fortified milk, eggs, salmon, and light tuna.

MORNING, NOON, OR NIGHT— WHAT TIME IS BEST TO FEED BABY?

At first, your baby will be eating solid foods just once or twice a day. For new foods, it's best to serve them in the morning or early afternoon, just not right before a nap. You'll want to observe your baby for two hours after eating a new food to look for signs of a food allergy, so before naps and before bed isn't ideal.

You also want to separate breast milk or formula feedings from solid food feedings. Your baby might not want to eat solid foods if they have just nursed or drunk from a bottle. Or, if your baby is very hungry, they might crave the familiarity of breast milk or formula. To increase the likelihood of your baby being willing to sit in the highchair and focus on eating, serve solid foods 30 minutes to one hour *after* your baby last nursed or had a bottle.

Around nine months old, your baby will be eating three meals a day: breakfast, lunch, and dinner. You can serve these around the same time that the rest of the family eats, still separating meals from breast milk or formula feedings by 30 minutes to one hour.

At around 12 months old, you can start adding one to two snacks per day in between meals. This means that your baby will have a meal or snack every two to three hours. This will remain their schedule for the foreseeable future.

Keep these tips in mind to create safe and stress-free mealtimes:

Safe seating: Your baby should always be seated upright and secured in a highchair during meals. Eating while crawling, walking, or in a car seat or stroller can increase the risk of choking.

Avoid distractions: Loud background noise (such as the TV or radio) can distract your baby during mealtimes and makes it more difficult to focus on the delicious food you've made for them.

Be a responsive feeder: Being a responsive feeder helps your baby develop healthy eating habits. It means that you provide the food and let your baby decide how much they need to eat. Babies can naturally regulate their food intake; they know best how much food their bodies need. It's completely normal that they eat a lot some meals, while at others they eat very little. It all averages out.

Recognize the signs that your baby is *hungry* (leans toward food with an open mouth, gets excited at the sight of food) and the signs that your baby is *full* (pushes food away, turns their head away from food, closes their mouth when you offer food, plays with their food). Honor these signs. Don't force your baby to finish their meal and don't say no if they want more.

Encourage self-feeding: Self-feeding helps your baby control the amount of food they eat, so they eat just enough, but not too much. Let your baby use all their senses to eat. Strip them down to just their diaper, give them a small bowl of food, and let them get messy! Instead of traditional spoon-feeding, try placing a spoon loaded with food on your baby's tray and let them pick it up and try to feed themselves.

RECOGNIZING FOOD REACTIONS

Even though food allergies and other food reactions are unlikely, it can be all you think about for those first few bites of a new food. The first time I gave my daughter peanut butter, I just sat there, holding my breath, waiting for something to go wrong. Thankfully, nothing happened. But if a reaction does occur, it pays to be prepared so you can act quickly and confidently.

AVOID THESE FOODS THROUGHOUT BABY'S FIRST YEAR

Even though most foods are safe, there are some foods babies shouldn't have before their first birthday.

Honey may contain bacteria that can cause infant botulism, a serious condition that often requires hospitalization. Avoid all kinds of honey, even raw honey, and foods that include honey as an ingredient.

Cow's milk shouldn't be given as a drink because it's significantly lower in iron than breast milk or formula, it's difficult for babies to digest, and its high calcium content may inhibit the absorption of iron from other foods, which can result in iron-deficiency anemia. While other dairy foods are fine (like yogurt and cheese) and cow's milk is fine as an ingredient in foods, stick with breast milk, formula, and water to drink.

Fruit juice contributes to tooth decay and has fewer nutrients than whole fruit. The American Academy of Pediatrics recommends no fruit juice before one year old. After your baby turns one, limit fruit juice to no more than 4 ounces a day.

Salt and sugar should be limited. Too much salt can strain your baby's kidneys, while added sugar lacks nutritional value and can lead to tooth decay. Don't add salt to your baby's food and choose "low-sodium" varieties of packaged foods. Naturally sweet foods, such as fruit, are safe and delicious for babies.

Fish high in mercury, like albacore tuna, swordfish, mackerel, and tilefish are unsafe for babies and young children. Choose light tuna (skipjack), salmon, sardines, cod, and other low-mercury fish.

Choking hazards need to be avoided. The most common choking hazards for babies include pieces of raw or hard fruits and vegetables (such as apples, carrots, and cucumbers); whole, round fruits or vegetables (such as berries, cherries, grapes, and cherry tomatoes); raisins; whole or chopped nuts; large globs of peanut butter; large chunks of meat or cheese; chewy meats (such as hot dogs and sausages); hard snacks (such as chips, pretzels, and granola bars); and hard candies. Many of these foods remain choking hazards until age four or five.

GAGGING

Even though it's scary to watch, gagging is completely normal. Babies are born with a natural gag reflex, which starts to fade away at around six to eight months old. So if your baby gags, stay calm and let them work through it on their own. Don't pat them on the back or show that you're scared, as this can make it worse and increase the risk of choking.

CHOKING

Choking is often silent, as a baby's airway is partially or fully blocked. If your baby is coughing, stay close and let them try to cough the food out. But if your baby cannot breathe or make a sound, turn them facedown on your forearm or lap, support their head, and slap their back between the shoulder blades with your palm. Call 911 if needed. Be prepared and take an infant CPR class. See References (page 164) for a link to a video showing you how to help a choking infant or child.

ALLERGIES

While food allergies are unlikely, affecting only 7.6 percent of children younger than 18 years old, you should be on the lookout for signs of an allergic reaction. These eight foods account for about 90 percent of all food allergies in the US:

Milk	Shellfish	Wheat
Eggs	Tree nuts	Soy
Fish	Peanuts	

Symptoms of a food allergy can happen within a few minutes, or up to a few hours after eating a food. Not everyone experiences the same symptoms, but they can include:

Vomiting	Coughing, sneezing, or wheezing	Swelling of the lips, tongue, or face
Diarrhea		
Hives	Congestion or runny nose	Difficulty breathing
Eczema		

If your baby shows any of these signs of an allergic reaction, make an appointment with your pediatrician. However, if your baby has a serious reaction, such as swelling or trouble breathing, call 911 immediately.

INTOLERANCE

A food intolerance is different from an allergy and is not life-threatening. For adults, the most common food intolerance is lactose intolerance, although this is unlikely to occur in babies.

In babies, food intolerance may look like bloating, gas, or diarrhea after eating a food. If you think a certain food is causing this reaction, try avoiding that food for several days to see if the symptoms improve.

THEY JUST DON'T WANT TO EAT

What if your baby doesn't want to eat? It doesn't necessarily mean that something is wrong. There are any number of reasons why babies don't want to eat. Developmental causes may be at play, but your child could simply be tired, teething, or distracted. Don't force it. You can always try again later.

In some cases, developmental or sensory challenges can make it harder for babies to eat solid foods. If you have concerns, consult your pediatrician.

MANGO PURÉE, PAGE 42

CHAPTER 2

You don't need to be a professional chef to prepare delicious, healthy food for your baby. With the right tools and techniques, preparing homemade meals for your baby will be easy, safe, and fun.

The tips you'll learn in this chapter will be valuable well beyond the baby years. You'll learn how planning meals and cooking in large batches can save you time and money, what tools can help you cook and freeze foods with ease, and best practices for keeping your frozen food fresh and well organized. You'll also learn all the food safety basics for shopping, preparing, storing, and reheating foods, to make sure all the food you prepare for your baby—and the rest of the family—is safe to eat.

By the end of this chapter, you'll be ready to move on to the fun part: making your own baby food!

MEAL PLANNING

Meal planning is a simple strategy to save time and money while helping you enjoy stress-free meals. The meal plans in this book are designed to give your baby a survey of textures, flavors, and nutrients. Use these meal plans as a model for the future, swapping out some of your favorite foods or rearranging meals however you like.

Once your meal plan is set, making food ahead of time is how the magic happens. Even if you love to cook (like me!), it can be a real challenge to make food from scratch after a sleepless night, a long day at work, or even a normal Tuesday.

Invest a few weekend hours to save time during the week. The secret here? Making a dozen portions of baby food takes the same amount of time as a single portion. Even a double batch of dinner only takes a few extra minutes, so you can have one meal now and another later. Weeknight meals are a breeze when all you need to do is reheat and serve.

Meal planning also saves you money. When you cook large batches of food, you can buy a "value size" or "family pack" of that food at the grocery store, which is cheaper by weight than smaller packages. Once you have fresh, homemade meals in the freezer, expensive convenience foods like prepackaged baby food or takeout won't seem as attractive.

American families waste an average of $1,600 worth of food each year. It's not intentional, but when fruits and vegetables spoil, bread goes stale, and meat smells off, it ends up in the trash. By meal planning, you'll buy only the food you need, and you'll cook it and store it before it goes bad and needs to be tossed.

THE MAKE-AHEAD METHOD:
BATCH COOKING AND FREEZING

Baby food is ideal when prepared in bulk: Babies eat such small portions at each meal that cooking up to 15 or even 20 servings is totally manageable. In fact, each of the Stage 1 recipes in this book makes 16 servings, which fills one ice cube tray.

For storing your homemade baby food, the freezer is your friend. When you freeze food, you preserve its color, flavor, and nutrients. Frozen food is just as nutritious as fresh. Every recipe for your baby in this book can be stored in the freezer and reheated as needed.

The first set of recipes, Stage 1, are purées, made by steaming and blending foods with a little water until they are smooth and creamy. The easiest way to freeze these purées is in ice cube trays. Once they are fully frozen, you can easily transfer them into a freezer-safe zip-top bag.

Next, you'll move on to Stage 2 recipes, which are thicker and chunkier. You can use the same freezer method for Stage 2 as for Stage 1, freezing the baby food in an ice cube tray and transferring the frozen cubes to a zip-top bag for storage.

As your baby becomes a master chewer, you'll start to introduce Stage 3 recipes. While some of the Stage 3 foods (like smoothies and sauces) can be stored in ice cube trays, the finger foods in this section are best frozen in a large freezer-safe zip-top bag, and then individual items can be taken out and defrosted as needed.

BEST PRACTICES FOR FOOD PREPARATION

Above all else, practicing good food safety is essential to reducing the odds of your baby getting a foodborne illness (also known as food poisoning). Babies and children younger than five years old don't have a mature immune system to protect them from germs. Follow these tips to keep food safe for your baby and the rest of your family:

Shopping: Choose colorful fresh fruits and vegetables free of bruises, damage, or mushy spots. When shopping for raw meat, poultry, and sea-food, make sure the packaging is not torn or leaking and that the "Sell by" date has not passed. Choose cans that are not dented or bulging, as this could be a sign that bacteria is growing within.

Storing: Place raw meat, poultry, and seafood on a rimmed dish in the refrigerator so juices don't drip onto other foods. Store the rimmed dish on the lowest shelf of your refrigerator and freezer to keep them colder. Separate cooked and ready-to-eat foods from the raw food by storing them on a higher shelf. Use a refrigerator/freezer thermometer to make sure your refrigerator is 40°F or lower, and that your freezer is 0°F or lower.

Prepping: Clean your countertops, cutting boards, and utensils before you start to cook and after handling raw foods. Wash your hands with warm, soapy water for 20 seconds before cooking and after handling raw foods, and wash your hands and baby's hands before eating. Separate raw foods and cooked foods throughout the cooking process. Wash all fresh fruits and vegetables, even ones where you remove the peel (this is done to prevent the transfer of bacteria from the outside of the fruit to the inside of the fruit). Because of their immature immune systems, babies are more susceptible to foodborne illness, so proper washing is an important preventive step.

Cooking: Use a food thermometer to cook meat, poultry, seafood, and eggs to the proper internal temperature. Babies and young children should not eat any raw or undercooked foods. Cook fish to 145°F, meat to 160°F, and poultry and eggs to 165°F. See the Resources section (page 162) for more information on food safety from the Centers for Disease Control and Prevention (CDC) and FoodSafety.gov, a food safety blog run by the CDC and the U.S. Food and Drug Administration (FDA).

Serving: Serve your baby from a small bowl rather than a large container. Placing a spoon that was in your baby's mouth into a larger container can contaminate the food with germs, meaning any leftovers can't be saved. Don't let food sit out at room temperature for more than two hours, or more than one hour on a hot day.

Chilling: Store leftovers in the refrigerator for two to three days, and in the freezer for two to three months. Cool foods on the counter before refrigerating or freezing them (but not for longer than two hours), because placing hot foods in the refrigerator or freezer can raise the temperature of other foods and lead to bacterial growth.

Defrosting and Reheating: Defrost foods in the refrigerator, in a cold-water bath, or in the microwave. Don't defrost food on the counter, as bacteria is likely to grow. When reheating foods, heat thoroughly to 165°F, and then let cool before serving. If microwaving food, stir and let stand for at least 30 seconds so the heat can distribute.

SPECIAL TIPS FOR FREEZING

To help your frozen baby food stay fresh, defrost easily, and taste as delicious on the day it's served as the day it was made, try these tips:

Freeze individual portions: Defrosted food can't be refrozen, so freezing in individual portions allows you to reheat only what you need for that meal. All the baby food recipes in this book are meant to be frozen in individual portions, but you can also freeze the family meals in smaller portions, making it easy to reheat less when one parent is away or heat up an extra portion when Grandma comes to visit.

Let food cool before freezing it: Let food cool at room temperature for no more than two hours or in the refrigerator before placing it in the freezer. Freezing food that has cooled first creates smaller ice crystals and results in better-tasting food after it's been reheated. Placing hot food directly in the freezer can also affect the temperature of the surrounding food, which can lead to bacterial growth and affect the taste and texture of that food.

Remove as much air as possible: To prevent freezer burn, which is caused by exposure to air while frozen, remove as much air as possible in your storage container before freezing. While the food will still be safe to eat, freezer burn dries out the food, affecting its flavor and texture. If you have a vacuum sealer, use it to remove all the air from zip-top bags. Or use a straw to suck out the extra air from a zip-top bag (but avoid doing this with raw meat, poultry, or seafood). You can also wrap foods in plastic wrap, wax paper, or aluminum foil to create an airtight seal.

TOOLS FOR THE MAKE-AHEAD KITCHEN

You don't need any fancy gadgets to make your own baby food. A few simple tools will help make your time in the kitchen more efficient and relaxed. Here are some of the essentials, as well as some nice-to-have options, that you'll want to have on hand to be ready to make your own baby food.

Essential kitchen tools:

- **Blender** – If there's one item to invest in, it's a blender. A good blender means you can make smooth puréed baby food, frosty smoothies, and creamy soups with ease.

- **Food processor** – A good alternative if you don't have a blender, although it may take a little more processing time for smooth purées.
- **Immersion blender** – Also called a "stick blender," this is a good substitute if you don't have a blender or food processor. It may take longer and require more liquid to make a smooth purée.
- **Cutting boards** – I recommend having at least two cutting boards: one for raw meat, poultry, and fish, and one for fruits, vegetables, and cooked foods.
- **Chef's knife** – A big, sharp knife around 8 inches long makes it easy to cut through a large butternut squash or chop potatoes. Try a ceramic knife, which is lightweight and long-lasting.
- **Prep bowls** – Use a set of small prep bowls to organize all your ingredients for a recipe before you start to cook.
- **Rimmed baking sheet** – This is an essential oven tool for roasting and baking.
- **Spatula** – A flexible spatula is great for getting every drop of puréed baby food out of your blender or food processor.
- **Saucepot with lid** – Perfect for steaming fruits and vegetables and making soups and sauces. Invest in both medium (3 quarts) and large (4 to 6 quarts) sizes.
- **Steamer basket or insert** – Many pots come with their own steamer basket, which fits snugly on top and has holes in the bottom to let steam in. You can also buy a steamer insert, a metal or silicone bowl that sits inside your pot.
- **Meat thermometer** – Don't use the color or feel of meat to gauge if it's fully cooked. A digital thermometer is the most accurate way to make sure your baby's food is fully cooked and safe to eat.
- **Fridge/freezer thermometer** – Many newer refrigerators have built-in thermometers, but if yours doesn't, an inexpensive thermometer lets you know your refrigerator and freezer are at the right temperatures.

Nice-to-have kitchen tools:

- **Vacuum sealer** – To get the ultimate protection from freezer burn, use a vacuum sealer and remove every bit of air from the bag.

Slow cooker – Nothing beats coming home after a long day to find dinner hot and ready and waiting for you on the counter.

Coffee scoop – A standard coffee scoop is equal to 2 tablespoons, a good serving size for babies. Have an extra one on hand for easy portioning.

FREEZER-RELATED TOOLS YOU'LL NEED

It's just as easy to make a dozen portions of baby food as it is a single portion, so it's smart to prepare large batches and freeze them for later. Here are some essential tools to make your freezing process efficient and ensure your freezer meals come out as delicious as they were going in.

Ice cube trays – Choose either BPA-free plastic or silicone one-ounce-capacity ice cube trays. To make a one-month supply of baby food, you'll need at least six ice cube trays.

Wrapping – Plastic wrap, aluminum foil, and wax paper all help create an airtight seal and protect your food from freezer burn. It's perfect for wrapping individual items like muffins.

Freezer-safe zip-top bags – I use both gallon-size and quart-size freezer-safe bags. Quart-size bags hold one ice cube tray's worth of baby food perfectly, and gallon-size bags are excellent for dinners.

Freezer-safe storage containers – Freezer-safe glass or plastic storage containers are reusable and environmentally friendly. Look for containers that specify they are freezer-safe, have tight-fitting lids, and stack neatly.

Freezer-safe labels – Unlike other tape, special freezer labels will stick to your frozen bags and containers.

Permanent marker – Use a permanent marker to label your baby food containers with the date, name of the recipe, and reheating instructions.

Bag holders – Fill your zip-top bags quickly and easily with bag holders, which look and act like an extra set of hands to hold zip-top bags open for you and make them easier to fill.

STORAGE MADE SIMPLE

When meal prepping, organizing your freezer efficiently is key! A disorganized freezer can create more stress and make it harder to find and reheat the food that you lovingly prepared.

Before diving in, take some time to clean out your freezer. Cook or toss anything that's past its prime, freezer burned, or a straight-up UFO ("Unidentified Freezer Object"). Remove any ice buildup and use a freezer thermometer to ensure your freezer is 0°F or colder.

LABEL EVERYTHING

Use a permanent marker or freezer-safe label to keep track of all your frozen meals. You don't want to go through the effort to defrost and reheat a food only to realize it was the wrong one!

Include the recipe name, the date you made it, and the date it should be used by. Every recipe in this book gives the storage time. For family dinners, you might also want to include the number of servings in each bag, reheating instructions, or any garnishes or additional components to add to the final meal. If anyone in your household has allergies, include a note if the food is off-limits for them.

KEEP AN INVENTORY

Take a tip from restaurants and keep an inventory of all the freezer meals you have on hand. An inventory helps you prevent unnecessary shopping trips, use up food before it becomes freezer burned, and plan meals.

To create a freezer inventory, make a list of all the food in your freezer and the date it was frozen, and mark one slash "/" for each serving. As you cook, add each new food to the list. Then, as you eat, turn each "/" into an "X" to show that it was used up. Once you have only a few "/" left, you know it's time to cook more!

FREEZE FLAT

When freezing items in a zip-top bag, like a soup or a batch of meatballs, freezing flat helps you save space and stay organized. Flat bags stack neatly and are less likely to topple over whenever you open the freezer door.

Place filled zip-top bags on a baking sheet or cutting board before placing in the freezer. Once they are frozen solid, you can easily stack many bags on top of one another. Freezing flat also helps food freeze faster, which means that it will have a better texture when reheated.

STAY ORGANIZED

While zip-top bags are compact, your freezer can quickly become overrun with bags and containers, all slipping and sliding on top of one another.

Try organizing your frozen food by food group, including separate areas for fruits and vegetables, raw meats and fish (always store on a lower shelf than prepared foods), baked goods, and complete meals. Then place each group into larger organizing containers. Even better, choose different-colored containers or attach a label to the outside so it's easy to locate each type of food.

WHEN YOU'RE READY TO FEED BABY

Once you've cooked, cooled, and frozen your baby food, the final steps are to thaw, reheat, and serve it. You've already done most of the work to freeze your food properly and pack it in airtight containers, locking in the taste and texture. Now, it's time to thaw and reheat your food so it looks and tastes just as good as when it went into the freezer.

Continue your good food safety practices to prevent the growth of bacteria as you thaw and reheat your baby's meals. The key here is to heat the food to a temperature that will kill any foodborne illness, while letting it cool to a safe temperature that won't burn your baby's mouth.

HOW TO THAW SAFELY

There are three safe ways to thaw frozen food: in the refrigerator, in a cold-water bath, and in the microwave. Don't let frozen food thaw on the countertop. And I don't recommend cooking frozen raw meat, poultry, or seafood. Because it takes so long to cook, you may inadvertently under-cook it, which can lead to the growth of bacteria.

Thawing frozen food in the refrigerator is the easiest method but takes the most time. Place frozen raw meat, poultry, or seafood in a covered bowl or dish on the lowest shelf in your refrigerator. Thaw frozen cooked food in an airtight container, zip-top bag, or covered plate or bowl. When defrosting in the refrigerator, your food can stay refrigerated for up to one day before being cooked and eaten.

A quicker way to thaw frozen foods is in a cold-water bath. Submerge the frozen food stored in a zip-top bag or airtight container in a bowl or baking dish filed with cold water. Change the water every 30 minutes until the food is defrosted. Always defrost frozen raw meat, poultry, or seafood separately from frozen cooked food. Any food defrosted in a cold-water bath should be cooked and eaten immediately.

The quickest way to thaw frozen food is with the microwave. Place your frozen food on a microwave-safe plate or dish and defrost it using the "defrost" or "50 percent power" setting on your microwave. Rotate and separate the food periodically to help it defrost evenly. Food defrosted in the microwave should also be cooked and eaten immediately.

Keep in mind that some cooked frozen foods won't need to be thawed at all prior to reheating them. Baked goods like muffins, soups and sauces, and cooked meatballs will often thaw as they reheat, so there is no need to thaw them first. Each of the recipes in this book provides specific thawing and reheating instructions.

REHEATING

Reheat frozen food thoroughly to 165°F to make sure any bacteria are killed off before you serve it to your baby. It's better to overheat food and let it cool off than to underheat it, which risks harmful bacteria that could make you or your baby sick.

For Stage 1 (puréed) and Stage 2 (chunky) foods, the microwave is by far the easiest way to reheat them. Choose microwave-safe dishes made from glass, ceramic, or BPA-free plastic. Don't place any metal objects in the microwave. Many frozen Stage 1 and Stage 2 foods can be heated in as little as 30 seconds or up to 1 minute. Heat in 30-second increments, and after the microwave finishes, stir and let the food sit for at least 30 more seconds so the heat can evenly distribute. Stir again and let the food cool before serving.

After heating, if you find the is food too thick, add a spoonful of water, breast milk, or formula to thin it out. If you find the food is too runny, try adding another item to thicken it up, such as yogurt, oatmeal, mashed potatoes, or applesauce.

For Stage 3 (finger foods) and family meals, you can choose to reheat food in the microwave, in the oven, or on the stovetop. Foods that were originally baked in the oven (such as roasted vegetables, muffins, and baked fish) are often best when reheated in the oven. Many of these cooked foods can be reheated straight from the freezer—there's no need to defrost. For wetter foods, like soups, stews, and sauces, reheating in the microwave or on the stovetop is ideal.

Always test your baby's food before serving to make sure it's not too hot. The best way to test the temperature is to taste it using your own spoon, not your baby's spoon. The food should be lukewarm, around 100°F when using a thermometer.

IT'S TIME TO MAKE YOUR BABY'S FOOD

Grab your apron and settle your baby down for a nap, because it's time to get cooking! All the recipes in this book are easy and quick to prepare, and use fresh, wholesome ingredients available at most major grocery stores. You'll also find instructions for storing and reheating food.

Stage 1 recipes are creamy puréed foods to help your baby learn how to eat solid foods. Try the classic Applesauce (page 37), Sweet Potato Purée (page 45), and Oatmeal Cereal (page 49).

Stage 2 recipes help your baby learn how to chew by providing chunkier textures and more exciting flavor combinations. You'll want to serve yourself a portion of Tropical Chia Seed Pudding (page 72), Guacamole with Peas and Cilantro (page 78), and Lemon-Parsley Salmon (page 88).

Stage 3 recipes include sauces, smoothies, and soft finger foods to encourage your baby to feed themselves with that pincer grasp they are working so hard on! These aren't only for baby, though. The whole family can enjoy Carrot and Prune Muffins (page 110), Egg Cups with Spinach, Peppers, and Cheese (page 124), and Ginger-Garlic Beef Meatballs (page 125).

If there's one theme you'll pick up on when reading the recipes in this book, it's that babies don't need bland, boring food. In the first few months of your baby's life, you've already seen how curious they are about the world around them. And now with solid foods, you can continue to excite your little one by introducing bold flavors. Your favorite ingredients and tastes are great to introduce to them, too! Help your baby develop into an adventurous eater and build a strong connection to their family and culture.

ON-THE-GO SNACK FOODS STAGE BY STAGE

When you're running errands, traveling, or visiting friends and family, it's a good idea to have food for your baby ready to go. If traveling with refrigerated or frozen baby food, pack it in an insulated lunch bag with an ice pack to keep it at a safe temperature. But for those throw-it-in-your-bag-and-go kinds of days, pack these foods, which don't need to be refrigerated:

Stage 1 | Puréed Foods

- **Avocado or banana.** They come with their own convenient packaging! Simply open up an avocado or banana and mash with a fork until smooth.

- **Nut butters.** Look for single-serving packets of almond butter, peanut butter, or other nut butters. Choose unsweetened varieties and thin with water, breast milk, or formula before serving.

- **Applesauce.** Choose unsweetened applesauce in single-serving containers.

Stage 2 | Chunky Foods

- **Banana, avocado, berries, or kiwi.** Mash with a fork until mostly smooth.

- **Tuna or salmon.** Look for single-serving packets of low-sodium salmon or chunk light (skipjack) tuna without added seasonings. Mash with a fork until mostly smooth.

- **O-cereal.** Bring a small container of unsweetened O-cereal and let soak in water, breast milk, or formula until it softens.

Stage 3 | Finger Foods

- **Soft raw vegetables.** These can include avocado and cherry tomatoes. Cut the veggies into pieces about the size of a pea.

- **Fresh ripe fruit.** Consider packing banana, berries, peach, plum, seedless orange, or kiwi. Cut the fruit into pieces about the size of a pea, removing any tough, fibrous parts.

- **Crackers and teething biscuits.** See the recipes for Chickpea Crackers (page 112) and Teething Biscuits (page 108).

PART II

MAKE-AHEAD MEAL PLANS AND RECIPES BY STAGE

GREEN PEA PURÉE, PAGE 43; MANGO PURÉE, PAGE 42; BLACK BEAN PURÉE, PAGE 52

Baby, your table is ready! There are so many exciting "firsts" with your baby, and starting solids is one of the biggest.

This chapter gets you started with:

- A review of the signs that your baby is ready for solid foods.

- One four-week meal plan outlining exactly what to feed your baby during their first month of solid foods.

- A shopping list for all the ingredients you'll need this first month.

- Instructions on the appropriate serving size and how to safely store and defrost foods.

- Twenty Stage 1 recipes, featuring a variety of flavors, colors, and nutrients.

IS YOUR BABY READY FOR STAGE 1?

While you can (and should!) make all the recipes in this chapter ahead of time, wait until your baby is ready for solid foods to serve them.

Remember, most babies are ready for solid foods around six months old, but some might be a little younger; others might be a little older. Don't start sooner than four months old, as your baby's digestive system is too immature to handle solid foods at that age. Wait until you see all the signs of readiness. Many babies will show an interest in your food early on, but that shouldn't be your *only* sign to start serving solid foods.

Look for the physical and developmental signs your baby is ready for solid foods, including:

- **Good head control** – Your baby should be able to hold their head up easily for long periods.
- **Sit with support** – Your baby should be able to sit mostly on their own, with a little support as needed.
- **Loss of tongue thrust** – Your baby's tongue should be able to move food further into their mouth to swallow, not push it back out.
- **Interested in food** – Your baby should open their mouth to accept food. If you offer a spoonful of food and your baby turns or pushes it away, that may be a sign they're not quite ready.

Now is also a good time to touch base with your pediatrician to confirm your baby is ready for solid foods and discuss any questions or concerns you have.

HOW TO STORE, DEFROST, AND REHEAT STAGE 1 FOODS

The majority of recipes in this chapter use the same defrosting and reheating instructions: To use within 3 days, store in an airtight container and refrigerate. Or to store for up to 3 months, freeze in ice cube trays. Transfer the frozen cubes to a zip-top bag, label with the recipe name and date, and store. Defrost the frozen food in the refrigerator, in a cold-water bath, or in the microwave. Serve cold or heat in the microwave in 30-second increments, until heated thoroughly. Allow to cool before serving.

All the recipes in this meal plan are quick and easy to prepare. Make the recipes in the order in the table that follows to maximize your efficiency in the kitchen.

RECIPE NAME	PAGE NUMBER	SERVING SIZE	PREP TIME	COOK TIME
Sweet Potato Purée	45	2 tablespoons	5 minutes	45 minutes
Oatmeal Cereal	49	2 tablespoons	5 minutes	5 minutes
Barley Cereal	50	2 tablespoons	5 minutes	10 minutes
Applesauce	37	2 tablespoons	5 minutes	10 minutes
Blueberry Purée	41	2 tablespoons	5 minutes	5 minutes
Mango Purée	42	2 tablespoons	10 minutes	5 minutes
Green Pea Purée	43	2 tablespoons	5 minutes	10 minutes
Carrot Purée	44	2 tablespoons	5 minutes	15 minutes
Cauliflower Purée	47	2 tablespoons	5 minutes	10 minutes
Red Lentil Purée	53	2 tablespoons	5 minutes	20 minutes
Avocado Purée	55	2 tablespoons	5 minutes	-
Peanut Butter Purée	56	2 tablespoons	5 minutes	-

MEAL PLAN FOR STAGE 1

When your baby begins eating solid foods, introduce foods one at a time, two to three days apart, so if baby shows any signs of an allergic reaction, you'll be able to easily isolate the food that most likely caused it. Once your baby has tried a food several times without a reaction, you can introduce another new food, either by itself or paired with a food that they have already tried.

In addition to the Stage 1 recipes in this book, this month's meal plan includes plain whole-milk yogurt, full of calcium and healthy fats, and hardboiled egg yolks, which are packed with great nutrients like iron, vitamin D, and choline. They can't be frozen, but can be stored in the refrigerator for up to three days.

To start, serve your baby one meal a day, referred to here as "Breakfast." After a few weeks, you can add a second meal during the day, which is referred to here as "Lunch" but could also be served around dinnertime.

WEEK 1	MONDAY	TUESDAY	WEDNESDAY	
BREAKFAST	Avocado Purée	Sweet Potato Purée (page 45)	Sweet Potato Purée	

WEEK 2	MONDAY	TUESDAY	WEDNESDAY	
BREAKFAST	Applesauce (page 37)	Applesauce	Green Pea Purée (page 43)	

WEEK 3	MONDAY	TUESDAY	WEDNESDAY	
BREAKFAST	Barley Cereal	Mango Purée (page 42)	Mango Purée	

WEEK 4	MONDAY	TUESDAY	WEDNESDAY	
BREAKFAST	Blueberry Purée (page 41)	Blueberry Purée Barley Cereal	Cauliflower Purée (page 47)	
LUNCH	Sweet Potato Purée 1 hardboiled egg yolk, mashed with water, breast milk, or formula	Avocado Purée Green Pea Purée	Red Lentil Purée Mango Purée	

THURSDAY	FRIDAY	SATURDAY	SUNDAY
Red Lentil Purée (page 53)	Red Lentil Purée	Oatmeal Cereal (page 49)	Avocado Purée (page 55)

THURSDAY	FRIDAY	SATURDAY	SUNDAY
Green Pea Purée	1 hardboiled egg yolk, mashed with water, breast milk, or formula	1 hardboiled egg yolk, mashed with water, breast milk, or formula	Oatmeal Cereal

THURSDAY	FRIDAY	SATURDAY	SUNDAY
Carrot Purée (page 44)	Carrot Purée	2 tablespoons plain whole-milk yogurt	Barley Cereal (page 50)

THURSDAY	FRIDAY	SATURDAY	SUNDAY
Cauliflower Purée Carrot Purée	Peanut Butter Purée, (page 56)	Peanut Butter Purée	2 tablespoons plain whole-milk yogurt
Barley Cereal Applesauce	Oatmeal Cereal Blueberry Purée	Red Lentil Purée Mango Purée	Oatmeal Cereal Applesauce

SHOPPING LIST

PRODUCE

- Apples, 4 medium (about 1½ pounds)
- Avocados, 3 medium (about 1 pound)
- Blueberries, 4 cups (2 pints)
- Carrots, 5 medium (about 1 pound)
- Cauliflower, 1 medium head (about 1½ pounds)
- Mangos, 3 medium (about 1½ pounds)
- Sweet Potatoes, 2 medium (about 1 pound)

DAIRY AND EGGS

- Eggs, 3 large
- Yogurt, plain whole milk, ½ cup

FROZEN FOODS

- Green peas, 1 (13-ounce) bag

PANTRY ITEMS

- Barley, ½ cup
- Oats, old-fashioned rolled, ½ cup
- Peanut butter, creamy, unsalted natural, ⅔ cup
- Red lentils, dried, 1 cup

SPICES

- Cinnamon, ground (optional)
- Vanilla extract (optional)

APPLESAUCE

Prep time: 5 minutes   Cook time: 10 minutes
Makes: 16 (1-ounce) freezer cubes   Serving size: 2 tablespoons (1 cube)

Applesauce was one of the first foods I gave my daughter, and like most babies, she couldn't resist its natural sweetness and pleasant texture. Use any kind of apples you like—some of my favorites are Gala, Fuji, and Honeycrisp. Or combine several types of apples for unique flavor combinations. You can customize your applesauce even more with spices: Try adding ginger, cloves, or allspice for extra warmth and flavor.

4 medium apples, cored, peeled, and coarsely chopped (about 1½ pounds)

¼ teaspoon ground cinnamon (optional)

In a medium saucepan with a steamer basket or insert, bring about 1 inch of water to a simmer. Add the apples. Cover and simmer over low heat for 7 to 10 minutes, or until the apples are soft.

Remove from the heat and transfer the apples to a blender or food processor. Add the cinnamon (if using). Blend until smooth, adding a few tablespoons of water as needed to achieve the desired consistency.

Cool and serve, or transfer to an ice cube tray and freeze. (See page 32 for storage, defrosting, and reheating instructions.)

TIP: Pair applesauce with oatmeal, spinach, or even lentils. The vitamin C in apples will help your baby absorb the iron from these foods more easily.

PEAR PURÉE

Prep time: 5 minutes   Cook time: 5 minutes
Makes: 16 (1-ounce) freezer cubes   Serving size: 2 tablespoons (1 cube)

This Pear Purée is similar to Applesauce, but the flavor is subtler and more sophisticated. Try it with vanilla for a lovely warmth and slight sweetness. I recommend using Anjou, Bartlett, or Comice pears because they are soft and juicy when ripe. Most pears at the grocery store are still hard, so let them ripen on your counter until they give a little when you press into the narrow part of the pear with your thumb.

4 medium pears, cored, peeled, and coarsely chopped (about 1½ pounds)
¼ teaspoon vanilla extract (optional)

1. In a medium saucepan with a steamer basket or insert, bring about 1 inch of water to a simmer. Add the pears. Cover and simmer over low heat for 3 to 5 minutes, until the pears are soft.

2. Remove from the heat and transfer the pears to a blender or food processor. Add the vanilla (if using). Blend until smooth, adding a few tablespoons of water as needed to achieve the desired consistency.

3. Cool and serve, or transfer to an ice cube tray and freeze. (See page 32 for storage, defrosting, and reheating instructions.)

TIP: Pears are a natural constipation remedy. If your baby seems a little backed up, try adding Pear Purée to their next meal to help move things along.

PEACH PURÉE

Prep time: 10 minutes   Cook time: 1 minute
Makes: 16 (1-ounce) freezer cubes   Serving size: 2 tablespoons (1 cube)

Give your baby a taste of summer with this bright and sweet Peach Purée. Even in the dead of winter, you can use frozen peach slices to delight your baby's taste buds. Simply heat 4 cups of frozen peach slices in the microwave and blend with any released juices until smooth. Peaches are a great source of vitamin A for healthy eyesight, and vitamin C to help build your baby's immune system.

4 medium peaches (about 1½ pounds)

Bring a large pot of water to a boil. Place the peaches in the boiling water and cook for 30 seconds.

Using a slotted spoon, remove the peaches and transfer to a bowl of ice water. Let the peaches cool slightly, then use your hands to gently rub the skin off. Remove the pits and coarsely chop the peaches.

Transfer the peaches to a blender or food processor. Blend until smooth, adding a few tablespoons of water as needed to achieve the desired consistency.

Cool and serve, or transfer to an ice cube tray and freeze. (See page 32 for storage, defrosting, and reheating instructions.)

TIP: Pair peaches with oatmeal or barley cereal, yogurt, or another fruit like prunes or pears. Use any extra Peach Purée in Peaches and Cream Baked Oatmeal (page 107).

PRUNE PURÉE

Prep time: 5 minutes, plus 20 minutes to soak
Makes: 16 (1-ounce) freezer cubes   Serving size: 2 tablespoons (1 cube)

Prunes are simply dried plums, and babies love their irresistible sweetness. Not only can they help relieve painful constipation, they're also a good source of nutrients, including iron. Look for sulfite-free prunes, because some people experience allergic symptoms like hives or difficulty breathing after eating sulfites. And even if the package says they are pitted, do a quick check to make sure no pit pieces remain, because they can really damage your blender.

1½ cups pitted prunes

1. Put the prunes in a medium heat-safe bowl. Pour boiling water over the prunes to cover. Soak for 15 to 20 minutes, or until the prunes soften.

2. Strain the prunes, reserving the liquid, and transfer the prunes to a blender or food processor. Blend until smooth, adding 1 cup of the soaking liquid (plus more as needed) to achieve the desired consistency.

3. Cool and serve, or transfer to an ice cube tray and freeze. (See page 32 for storage, defrosting, and reheating instructions.)

TIP: Pair prunes with oatmeal or barley cereal, or with apples, pears, or carrots. Sweet prunes can also balance out more savory foods, such as spinach or chicken.

BLUEBERRY PURÉE

Prep time: 5 minutes   Cook time: 5 minutes
Makes: 16 (1-ounce) freezer cubes   Serving size: 2 tablespoons (1 cube)

Blueberries have been my daughter's favorite food since she was a baby. She made a good choice—blueberries contain lots of vitamin C and are very high in antioxidants, which help protect cells from damage. Since blueberries are a summer fruit, they'll be freshest and sweetest during those months. The rest of the year, frozen blueberries are the way to go. Instead of steaming frozen berries, simply heat them in the microwave and blend with any released juices.

4 cups fresh blueberries

In a medium saucepan with a steamer basket or insert, bring about 1 inch of water to a simmer. Add the blueberries. Cover and simmer over low heat for 3 to 5 minutes, or until the blueberries are soft.

Remove from the heat and transfer the blueberries to a blender or food processor. Blend until smooth, adding a few tablespoons of water as needed to achieve the desired consistency.

Cool and serve, or transfer to an ice cube tray and freeze. (See page 32 for storage, defrosting, and reheating instructions.)

TIP: If you come across wild blueberries (usually in the freezer section), try them! They taste amazing and have twice the antioxidants of regular blueberries.

MANGO PURÉE

Prep time: 10 minutes   Cook time: 5 minutes
Makes: 16 (1-ounce) freezer cubes   Serving size: 2 tablespoons (1 cube)

With a bright sweetness and creamy texture, Mango Purée is bound to become one of your baby's favorite foods. Mangos are an excellent source of nutrients, including vitamins A and C. They're also rich in vitamin B6, which helps your baby grow. You can easily substitute 1 (15-ounce) bag of frozen mango chunks, heated in the microwave and blended with any released juices. Mango Purée pairs well with any cereal, yogurt, black beans, or avocado.

3 mangos, pitted, peeled, and coarsely chopped (about 1½ pounds) ·

1. In a medium saucepan with a steamer basket or insert, bring about 1 inch of water to a simmer. Add the mangos. Cover and simmer over low heat for 3 to 5 minutes, or until the mangos are soft.

2. Remove from the heat and transfer the mangos to a blender or food processor. Blend until smooth, adding a few tablespoons of water as needed to achieve the desired consistency.

3. Cool and serve, or transfer to an ice cube tray and freeze. (See page 32 for storage, defrosting, and reheating instructions.)

TIP: To cut a mango, slice alongside the long, flat pit that runs down the middle of the fruit. Use a spoon to scoop out the flesh.

GREEN PEA PURÉE

Prep time: 5 minutes   Cook time: 10 minutes
Makes: 16 (1-ounce) freezer cubes   Serving size: 2 tablespoons (1 cube)

With the taste of a vegetable but the nutrition of a bean, green peas are the perfect powerhouse for your baby. Green peas are technically a legume, like beans and lentils, so they are a great source of iron and protein. What's more, their natural sweetness makes them easy for babies to love. I recommend using frozen peas for this recipe; they're more affordable and so much easier to use than fresh peas that need to be shelled.

1 (13-ounce) package frozen green peas
½ cup water

In a medium saucepan with a steamer basket or insert, bring about 1 inch of water to a simmer. Add the peas. Cover and simmer over low heat for 7 to 10 minutes, or until the peas are heated through.

Remove from the heat and transfer the peas to a blender or food processor. Blend until smooth, adding ½ cup of water (plus more as needed) to achieve the desired consistency.

Cool and serve, or transfer to an ice cube tray and freeze. (See page 32 for storage, defrosting, and reheating instructions.)

TIP: To help your baby absorb iron from the peas, pair them with a food high in vitamin C. There are plenty of options! Try mangos, berries, apples, cauliflower, or sweet potato.

CARROT PURÉE

Prep time: 5 minutes   Cook time: 15 minutes
Makes: 16 (1-ounce) freezer cubes   Serving size: 2 tablespoons (1 cube)

Carrots are a classic first food for babies—for good reason. Carrots have a natural sweetness that babies love, plus they are full of nutrients such as vitamin A to support your baby's eyesight, and antioxidants such as beta-carotene to help keep your baby's cells healthy. Be on the lookout for multicolored carrots—the red, yellow, white, and purple varieties are becoming more widely available. Each color of carrot has its own unique combination of vitamins and antioxidants.

5 medium carrots, peeled and coarsely chopped (about 1 pound)
½ cup water

1. In a medium saucepan with a steamer basket or insert, bring about 1 inch of water to a simmer. Add the carrots. Cover and simmer over low heat for 10 to 15 minutes, or until the carrots are soft.

2. Remove from the heat and transfer the carrots to a blender or food processor. Blend until smooth, adding ½ cup of water (plus more as needed) to achieve the desired consistency.

3. Cool and serve, or transfer to an ice cube tray and freeze. (See page 32 for storage, defrosting, and reheating instructions.)

TIP: Carrots pair well with every food group: fruits, vegetables, grains, and proteins. Try them with apples, prunes, cauliflower, quinoa, lentils, or chicken.

SWEET POTATO PURÉE

Prep time: 5 minutes   Cook time: 45 minutes
Makes: 16 (1-ounce) freezer cubes   Serving size: 2 tablespoons (1 cube)

If the bright orange color doesn't mesmerize your baby from the first bite, then the sweet flavor and fluffy texture is bound to capture their taste buds. Sweet potatoes are full of fiber and vitamin A, plus potassium to keep baby's muscles strong and blood pressure healthy. You could choose to steam sweet potatoes following the same directions as Carrot Purée (page 44), but if you've got the time, baking is a bit easier.

2 medium sweet potatoes
  (about 1 pound)
½ cup water

Preheat the oven to 425°F. Line a rimmed baking sheet with aluminum foil or parchment paper.

Prick the sweet potatoes all over with a fork. Place the sweet potatoes on the prepared baking sheet and bake for about 45 minutes, or until soft.

Remove from the oven and let cool slightly. Use a spoon to scoop the cooked sweet potato flesh into a medium bowl. Use a fork or potato masher to mash the sweet potato until smooth, adding ½ cup of water (plus more as needed) to achieve the desired consistency.

Cool and serve, or transfer to an ice cube tray and freeze. (See page 32 for storage, defrosting, and reheating instructions.)

TIP: Because sweet potatoes have a naturally thick and fluffy texture, they balance out thinner purées nicely. Try sweet potatoes with blueberries, spinach, or applesauce.

BUTTERNUT SQUASH PURÉE

Prep time: 5 minutes | Cook time: 45 minutes
Makes: 16 (1-ounce) freezer cubes | Serving size: 2 tablespoons (1 cube)

Butternut squash is full of nutrients to support your baby's growth and development. It has vitamins A and C, magnesium for growing strong bones, and more potassium than a banana. This is a great recipe to make in tandem with the Sweet Potato Purée (page 45) because they bake at the same temperature. And if you have a large squash, use the extra purée to make Butternut Squash Mac 'n' Cheese (page 138).

1 medium butternut squash
  (about 2 pounds)
½ cup water

1. Preheat the oven to 425°F. Line a rimmed baking sheet with parchment paper.

2. Remove the ends and cut the butternut squash in half lengthwise. Scoop out and discard the seeds.

3. Place the squash, cut-side down, on the baking sheet. Bake for 30 to 45 minutes, or until soft. Remove from the oven and let it cool.

4. When cool enough to handle, use a spoon to scoop the cooked squash flesh out from the peel, and transfer to a blender or food processor. Blend until smooth, adding ½ cup of water (plus more as needed) to achieve the desired consistency.

5. Cool and serve, or transfer to an ice cube tray and freeze. (See page 32 for storage, defrosting, and reheating instructions.)

TIP: Butternut squash pairs well with green peas, lentils, or black beans. Its sweet flavor also goes nicely with fruits such as apples, pears, or mangos.

CAULIFLOWER PURÉE

Prep time: 5 minutes   Cook time: 10 minutes
Makes: 16 (1-ounce) freezer cubes   Serving size: 2 tablespoons (1 cube)

Cauliflower may seem like a plain and boring vegetable, but it's actually packed with nutrition. It's a good source of fiber, vitamin B6, vitamin C, and antioxidants to keep cells healthy. Keep an eye out for the other varieties of cauliflower, like purple, yellow, and green—they are all delicious and packed with nutrients. Let your baby explore the raw cauliflower by feeling the bumpy texture and looking at all the beautiful bright colors.

1 medium head fresh cauliflower, cored and coarsely chopped (about 1½ pounds)

½ cup water

In a medium saucepan with a steamer basket or insert, bring about 1 inch of water to a simmer. Add the cauliflower. Cover and simmer over low heat for 7 to 10 minutes, or until the cauliflower is soft.

Remove from the heat and transfer the cauliflower to a blender or food processor. Blend until smooth, adding ½ cup of water (plus more as needed) to achieve the desired consistency.

Cool and serve, or transfer to an ice cube tray and freeze. (See page 32 for storage, defrosting, and reheating instructions.)

TIP: Because of its mild flavor, cauliflower pairs well with sweet or savory foods. Try it with sweet mangos and peaches, or with savory spinach, lentils, and chicken.

SPINACH PURÉE

Prep time: 5 minutes   Cook time: 5 minutes
Makes: 16 (1-ounce) freezer cubes   Serving size: 2 tablespoons (1 cube)

Spinach has a soft texture and not-too-bitter flavor that makes it a great first leafy green vegetable for your baby. Plus, it's full of the good stuff: iron, vitamin A, and folate to support the growth and development of healthy blood cells. This recipe uses fresh spinach, but you can easily substitute frozen. Warm a 10-ounce bag of frozen spinach in the microwave until heated through, and then blend along with any released liquid.

1 (16-ounce) bag fresh
   spinach leaves

1. In a medium saucepan with a steamer basket or insert, bring about 1 inch of water to a simmer. Add the spinach. Cover and simmer over low heat for 3 to 5 minutes, or until the spinach has wilted.

2. Remove from the heat and transfer the spinach to a blender or food processor. Blend until smooth, adding a few tablespoons of water as needed to achieve the desired consistency.

3. Cool and serve, or transfer to an ice cube tray and freeze. (See page 32 for storage, defrosting, and reheating instructions.)

TIP: Because spinach can have a slightly bitter flavor, balance it out by pairing it with sweet fruits and vegetables, such as sweet potatoes, mangos, butternut squash, or apples.

OATMEAL CEREAL

Prep time: 5 minutes   Cook time: 5 minutes
Makes: 16 (1-ounce) freezer cubes   Serving size: 2 tablespoons (1 cube)

Oatmeal cereal is a classic first baby food because it's warm, creamy, and hearty. Oats contain protein, fiber, iron, and phosphorus, which helps grow strong bones and teeth. In this recipe, process the oats first to make oat flour, then cook with water. You can easily make a double or triple batch of oat flour and save the extra to make Teething Biscuits (page 108), or to bring with you while traveling.

½ cup old-fashioned
rolled oats
2 cups water

In a food processor or blender, pulse the oats until you have a fine powder/flour.

In a medium saucepan, combine the oat flour and water and bring to a boil over medium heat. Cook, stirring frequently, for 3 to 5 minutes, or until bubbly and thick. For a thinner consistency, add more water a few tablespoons at a time. For a thicker consistency, continue to cook, stirring frequently.

Cool and serve, or transfer to an ice cube tray and freeze.

TIP: Oatmeal cereal pairs with fruits such as pears and mangos, vegetables such as carrots and peas, and even protein such as chicken or lentils. It's also wonderful with spices like cinnamon, cloves, and ginger.

TIP: If you want to save even more time, grind up extra oats and store the dry oat flour in an airtight container in the pantry for up to 6 months. See page 32 for Oatmeal Cereal storage, defrosting, and reheating instructions.

BARLEY CEREAL

Prep time: 5 minutes   Cook time: 10 minutes
Makes: 16 (1-ounce) freezer cubes   Serving size: 2 tablespoons (1 cube)

Barley is a simple and healthy cereal to make for your baby. It has a nutty flavor that complements vegetables, meat, and beans. Like other whole grains, barley contains iron, a mineral prominent in red blood cells to help carry oxygen throughout your baby's body. Look for barley in your local supermarket near the dried beans and rice. As with oatmeal, you can make a double or triple batch of barley flour and save the extra for another recipe or for traveling.

½ cup barley
3 cups water

1. In a food processor or blender, pulse the barley until you have a fine powder/flour.

2. In a medium saucepan, combine the barley flour and water and bring to a boil over medium heat. Cook, stirring frequently, for 7 to 10 minutes, or until bubbly and thick. For a thinner consistency, add more water a few tablespoons at a time. For a thicker consistency, continue to cook, stirring frequently.

3. Cool and serve, or transfer to an ice cube tray and freeze.

TIP: Pair barley cereal with peaches, prunes, butternut squash, or chicken. You can also combine barley flour with oat flour and quinoa to make Multigrain Cereal (page 70).

TIP: Store any extra dry barley flour in an airtight container in the pantry for up to 6 months. See page 32 for Barley Cereal storage, defrosting, and reheating instructions.

QUINOA CEREAL

Prep time: 5 minutes   Cook time: 20 minutes
Makes: 16 (1-ounce) freezer cubes   Serving size: 2 tablespoons (1 cube)

Quinoa is a nutrient-rich food from South America with a nutty flavor and fluffy texture. Even though it's technically a seed, it cooks up like a grain and has similar nutrition. Quinoa is a good source of iron, as well as zinc, which is essential for growth and keeping your baby's immune system strong. Need to double or triple this cereal? Easy. Cook 1 part quinoa in 2 parts water. Save the extra cooked quinoa for your own dinner.

½ cup quinoa, rinsed
1½ cups water, divided

In a small saucepan, combine the quinoa and 1 cup of water and bring to a boil over medium heat. Reduce heat to low, cover and cook for 10 to 15 minutes, or until all the water is absorbed. Turn off the heat and let sit, covered, for 5 additional minutes.

Transfer the quinoa to a blender or food processor. Blend until smooth, adding the remaining ½ cup water (plus more as needed) to achieve the desired consistency.

Cool and serve, or transfer to an ice cube tray and freeze. (See page 32 for storage, defrosting, and reheating instructions.)

TIP: Because quinoa has a stronger flavor than oats or barley, it's nice to balance it out with sweet foods, such as mangos, prunes, carrots, or butternut squash.

BLACK BEAN PURÉE

Prep time: 5 minutes   Cook time: 1½ hours
Makes: 16 (1-ounce) freezer cubes   Serving size: 2 tablespoons (1 cube)

All beans make wonderful baby foods—they have a smooth texture and mild flavor, and are full of nutrients like iron and fiber. This recipe uses black beans, which, unlike other beans, don't need to be soaked before cooking. If you've never cooked dried beans before, it's worth the effort. In a pinch, low-sodium canned beans work very well. Drain and rinse the canned beans, add them to a saucepan and fill with enough water to just cover them, and boil for about 5 minutes, or until heated through.

1 cup dried black beans, picked over and rinsed

1. Place the beans in a medium saucepot and cover with water by several inches. Cover, bring to a simmer, and cook, stirring occasionally, for 1 to 1½ hours, until the beans are soft.

2. Strain the beans, reserving the liquid. Transfer the beans and 1 cup of the cooking liquid to a blender or food processor. Blend until smooth, adding a few additional tablespoons of water as needed to achieve the desired consistency.

3. Cool and serve, or transfer to an ice cube tray and freeze. (See page 32 for storage, defrosting, and reheating instructions.)

TIP: Let the thick texture of black beans offset a thinner purée, like spinach or blueberry. Black beans also taste great with mangos, cauliflower, or butternut squash.

RED LENTIL PURÉE

Prep time: 5 minutes   Cook time: 20 minutes
Makes: 16 (1-ounce) freezer cubes   Serving size: 2 tablespoons (1 cube)

Like all legumes, lentils are a great source of iron and protein, as well as antioxidants and fiber, which support good digestion. For this recipe, I recommend red lentils, which naturally break down and get mushy as they cook. You can easily substitute green or brown lentils, but save the firm French lentils for when your baby is a bit older. Leftover red lentil purée works great to thicken up a soup or stew. Try it in Creamy Tomato Basil Soup with Lentils (page 135).

1 cup dried red lentils, picked over and rinsed

Place the lentils in a medium saucepot and cover with water by several inches. Cover, bring to a simmer, and cook, stirring occasionally, for about 20 minutes, or until the lentils are soft.

Strain the lentils, reserving the liquid. Transfer the lentils and ½ cup of the cooking liquid to a blender or food processor. Blend until smooth, adding a few additional tablespoons of water as needed to achieve the desired consistency.

Cool and serve, or transfer to an ice cube tray and freeze. (See page 32 for storage, defrosting, and reheating instructions.)

TIP: Pair lentils with any fruit or vegetable purée. Some of my favorite flavor combinations are lentils with applesauce, pears, butternut squash, or cauliflower.

CHICKEN PURÉE

Prep time: 5 minutes   Cook time: 10 minutes
Makes: 16 (1-ounce) freezer cubes   Serving size: 2 tablespoons (1 cube)

Many parents are now serving chicken as one of their baby's first foods. Chicken is a good source of iron, and the iron found in animal foods is more easily absorbed than the iron found in plants. Plus, the protein and fat in chicken help fuel your baby's rapid growth. This recipe uses chicken thighs because dark meat chicken is higher in iron and stays moist during cooking, making it easier to purée than chicken breast.

3 boneless, skinless chicken thighs, cut into 1-inch pieces (about ¾ pound)
½ cup water

1. In a medium saucepan with a steamer basket or insert, bring about 1 inch of water to a simmer. Add the chicken. Cover and simmer over low heat for 7 to 10 minutes, or until the chicken is cooked through and a thermometer registers 165°F.

2. Remove from the heat and transfer the chicken to a blender or food processor. Blend until smooth, adding ½ cup of water (plus more as needed) to achieve the desired consistency.

3. Cool and serve, or transfer to an ice cube tray and freeze.

TIP: Chicken pairs well with sweet or savory foods. Try it with apples or pears, or more classic combinations like barley, carrots, or green peas.

STORAGE: To use within 2 days, store in an airtight container and refrigerate. Or to store for up to 2 months, freeze in ice cube trays. Transfer the frozen cubes to a zip-top bag, label with the recipe name and date, and store. Defrost the frozen Chicken Purée in the refrigerator, in a cold-water bath, or in the microwave. Heat in the microwave in 30-second increments, until heated to 165°F. Allow to cool before serving.

AVOCADO PURÉE

Prep time: 5 minutes
Makes: 16 (1-ounce) freezer cubes   Serving size: 2 tablespoons (1 cube)

Avocado was the first food I fed my daughter, and now it's one of her favorites. I chose avocados as her first food because they're a great source of healthy fats and nutrients such as fiber, potassium, and vitamin C. Choose a ripe avocado that gives slightly when you press it with your thumb. When refrigerating Avocado Purée to use within 3 days, prevent it from browning by wrapping tightly with plastic wrap or squeezing a little lemon juice over the top.

3 ripe avocados, pitted
 (about 1 pound)

Scoop the avocado flesh into a medium bowl. Discard the skins. Use a fork or potato masher to mash the avocado until smooth.

Serve immediately, refrigerate, or freeze.

TIP: Pair avocado with mangos, blueberries, spinach, or chicken. You can also use leftover Avocado Purée to make Guacamole with Peas and Cilantro (page 78).

STORAGE: To use within 3 days, store in an airtight container and refrigerate. Or to store for up to 3 months, freeze in ice cube trays. Transfer the frozen cubes to a zip-top bag, label with the recipe name and date, and store. Defrost the frozen avocado purée in the refrigerator or in a cold-water bath. Serve cool. Microwaving is not recommended.

PEANUT BUTTER PURÉE

Prep time: 5 minutes
Makes: 16 (1-ounce) freezer cubes   Serving size: 2 tablespoons (1 cube)

It can be really scary to introduce a food like peanuts to your baby, but try not to worry. Research shows that for most babies, introducing peanut-containing foods early and often can actually help prevent a peanut allergy. Talk to your pediatrician first to make sure there's no reason to delay. When serving peanut butter for the first time, start with a tiny amount, wait 10 minutes, and if there is no reaction, slowly offer the rest.

⅔ cup creamy, unsalted natural peanut butter

1⅓ cup fruit or vegetable purée, such as Applesauce (page 37), Pear Purée (page 38), or Sweet Potato Purée (page 45)

1. In a small bowl, combine the peanut butter with the fruit or vegetable purée. Mix until well combined.

2. Serve immediately, or transfer to an ice cube tray and freeze. (See page 32 for storage, defrosting, and reheating instructions.)

TIP: Pair peanut butter with a fruit or vegetable that your baby has already tolerated, so if there is a reaction, you'll know it was as a result of the peanuts.

PEANUT BUTTER PURÉE, PAGE 56; CARROT PURÉE, PAGE 44; BLUEBERRY PURÉE, PAGE 41

LEMON-PARSLEY SALMON, PAGE 88; VERY BERRY SMOOTHIE, PAGE 73; CURRIED CAULIFLOWER AND CHICKPEAS, PAGE 83; GUACAMOLE WITH PEAS AND CILANTRO, PAGE 78

Now that your baby has become comfortable with Stage 1 foods, it's time to introduce Stage 2 foods, with thicker textures that serve as the bridge between creamy puréed foods and soft finger foods.

This stage also welcomes new ingredients and more complex flavors. Say hello to soft shredded meats and fish; herbs and spices such as thyme, cumin, and curry; and bright accents like lemon, garlic, and ginger. Your baby is maturing, and so is the repertoire!

Like chapter 3, this chapter includes a four-week meal plan along with its shopping list, outlining a month's worth of Stage 2 meals to help bring your baby one step closer to table foods.

IS YOUR BABY READY FOR STAGE 2?

There's no specific date at which to switch from Stage 1 to Stage 2 foods; instead, it happens gradually. Stage 2 foods let your baby practice chewing and handling different textures, and while it may be difficult at first, they'll soon master these skills.

Begin offering Stage 2 foods as soon as your baby shows signs they are ready. It will happen quicker than you expect. Some babies are ready only a few weeks after starting solid foods. The longer you wait, the more dependent your baby may become on the consistency of purées and be more resistant to try new textures, so don't be shy.

It's normal for babies to gag more often when transitioning to Stage 2 foods. It's all a part of the learning process. Try and stay calm so you don't scare your baby and cause them to choke. As long as your baby isn't gagging continually and is generally happy during meals, there's no cause for concern.

Look for these four signs that your baby is ready to transition to Stage 2 foods:

- **Demonstrating better mouth control** – Your baby should swallow puréed foods without much difficulty.

- **Closing lips around spoon** – Your baby should close their lips around a spoon.

- **Practicing chewing** – Your baby should start to position food between their jaws and practice a chewing motion.

- **Starting to self-feed** – Your baby is likely showing an interest in feeding themselves using their hands or a spoon.

With the exception of the Root Veggie Beef Stew and the Chicken and Sweet Potato Stew, which each cook for hours in a slow cooker, you can prepare all the recipes for this meal plan in several hours, spread out over a few days or a weekend. Make the recipes in the order in the table that follows to maximize your efficiency in the kitchen.

RECIPE NAME	PAGE NUMBER	SERVING SIZE	PREP TIME	COOK TIME
Root Veggie Beef Stew	89	¼ cup	10 minutes	4 to 8 hours
Baby's First Pumpkin Pie	71	¼ cup	5 minutes	45 minutes
Mashed Sweet Potatoes and Banana	79	¼ cup	5 minutes	45 minutes
Mashed Eggplant with Garlic	82	¼ cup	10 minutes	40 minutes
Mashed Roasted Zucchini with Thyme	80	¼ cup	10 minutes	20 minutes
Multigrain Cereal	70	¼ cup	5 minutes	15 minutes
Baked Apples and Pears	77	¼ cup	10 minutes	45 minutes
Tropical Chia Seed Pudding	72	2 tablespoons	5 minutes, plus 30 minutes to set	-
Chunky Carrots and Broccoli with Ginger	75	¼ cup	10 minutes	15 minutes
Guacamole with Peas and Cilantro	78	¼ cup	10 minutes	10 minutes
Creamed Spinach with White Beans	84	¼ cup	5 minutes	10 minutes
Lemon-Parsley Salmon	88	2 tablespoons	5 minutes	15 minutes
Chunky Green Beans with Lemon	81	¼ cup	5 minutes	15 minutes

RECIPE NAME	PAGE NUMBER	SERVING SIZE	PREP TIME	COOK TIME
Butternut Squash and Lentil Stew	85	¼ cup	10 minutes	20 minutes
Curried Cauliflower and Chickpeas	83	¼ cup	5 minutes	10 minutes
Mashed Potatoes with Bell Pepper and Sardines	86	¼ cup	10 minutes	15 minutes
Very Berry Smoothie	73	¼ cup	5 minutes	-
Cherry Almond Smoothie	74	¼ cup	5 minutes	-
Mashed Kiwi and Banana	76	¼ cup	5 minutes	-
Chicken and Sweet Potato Stew	90	¼ cup	5 minutes	4 to 8 hours

HOW TO STORE, DEFROST, AND REHEAT STAGE 2 FOODS

The majority of recipes in this chapter use the same defrosting and reheating instructions: To use within 3 days, store in an airtight container and refrigerate. Or to store for up to 3 months, freeze in ice cube trays. Transfer the frozen cubes to a zip-top bag, label with the recipe name and date, and store. Defrost the frozen food in the refrigerator, in a cold-water bath, or in the microwave. Serve cold or heat in the microwave in 30-second increments, until heated thoroughly. Allow to cool before serving.

MEAL PLAN FOR STAGE 2

In addition to the recipes in this section, you can serve your baby fully cooked scrambled egg, well-cooked small pasta (like orzo or stars), and plain whole-milk yogurt. Gradually increase the amount you serve at each meal, based on your baby's appetite.

WEEK 1	MONDAY	TUESDAY	WEDNESDAY
BREAKFAST	½ egg, scrambled Guacamole with Peas and Cilantro (page 78)	Tropical Chia Seed Pudding (page 72) Mashed Kiwi and Banana (page 76)	Very Berry Smoothie (page 73) Multigrain Cereal 2 teaspoons creamy unsalted natural peanut butter
LUNCH	Baby's First Pumpkin Pie (page 71) Multigrain Cereal	Root Veggie Beef Stew (page 89) Chunky Green Beans with Lemon (page 81)	Chicken and Sweet Potato Stew Chunky Carrots and Broccoli with Ginger
DINNER	Chicken and Sweet Potato Stew (page 90) Mashed Roasted Zucchini with Thyme (page 80)	Curried Cauliflower and Chickpeas (page 83) ¼ cup mashed avocado ¼ cup cooked pasta	Butternut Squash and Lentil Stew Baked Apples and Pears

WEEK 2	MONDAY	TUESDAY	WEDNESDAY
BREAKFAST	Mashed Kiwi and Banana ¼ cup plain whole-milk yogurt 2 teaspoons creamy unsalted natural peanut butter	½ egg, scrambled Guacamole with Peas and Cilantro Multigrain Cereal	Cherry Almond Smoothie ¼ cup plain whole-milk yogurt
LUNCH	Mashed Potatoes with Bell Pepper and Sardines Mashed Eggplant with Garlic	Tropical Chia Seed Pudding Baked Apples and Pears	Creamed Spinach with White Beans ¼ cup cooked pasta Baby's First Pumpkin Pie
DINNER	Root Veggie Beef Stew Mashed Roasted Zucchini with Thyme ¼ cup cooked pasta	Lemon-Parsley Salmon Chunky Carrots and Broccoli with Ginger	Chicken and Sweet Potato Stew Chunky Green Beans with Lemon

	THURSDAY	FRIDAY	SATURDAY	SUNDAY
	½ egg, scrambled Mashed Sweet Potatoes and Banana (page 79)	Multigrain Cereal Baby's First Pumpkin Pie	Cherry Almond Smoothie (page 74) ¼ cup plain whole-milk yogurt	Multigrain Cereal (page 70) Baked Apples and Pears (page 77) 2 teaspoons creamy unsalted natural peanut butter
	Lemon-Parsley Salmon Chunky Green Beans with Lemon ¼ cup cooked pasta	Curried Cauliflower and Chickpeas Mashed Eggplant with Garlic	Chicken and Sweet Potato Stew Chunky Green Beans with Lemon	Butternut Squash and Lentil Stew (page 85) Mashed Eggplant with Garlic (page 82)
	Root Veggie Beef Stew Mashed Roasted Zucchini with Thyme	Mashed Potatoes with Bell Pepper and Sardines (page 86) ¼ cup mashed avocado	Creamed Spinach with White Beans (page 84) ½ egg, scrambled ¼ cup cooked pasta	Lemon-Parsley Salmon (page 88) Chunky Carrots and Broccoli with Ginger (page 75)

	THURSDAY	FRIDAY	SATURDAY	SUNDAY
	Multigrain Cereal Mashed Kiwi and Banana 2 teaspoons creamy unsalted natural peanut butter	½ egg, scrambled Guacamole with Peas and Cilantro	Baby's First Pumpkin Pie ¼ cup plain whole-milk yogurt	Tropical Chia Seed Pudding Very Berry Smoothie
	Root Veggie Beef Stew Mashed Roasted Zucchini with Thyme	Tropical Chia Seed Pudding Very Berry Smoothie	Chicken and Sweet Potato Stew Mashed Eggplant with Garlic	Multigrain Cereal Mashed Sweet Potatoes and Banana
	Mashed Potatoes with Bell Pepper and Sardines Mashed Eggplant with Garlic	Butternut Squash and Lentil Stew Chunky Carrots and Broccoli with Ginger Multigrain Cereal	Curried Cauliflower and Chickpeas Mashed Roasted Zucchini with Thyme ¼ cup cooked pasta	Curried Cauliflower and Chickpeas ¼ cup mashed avocado

WEEK 3	MONDAY	TUESDAY	WEDNESDAY
BREAKFAST	½ egg, scrambled Guacamole with Peas and Cilantro	Butternut Squash and Lentil Stew Baked Apples and Pears	Multigrain Cereal Mashed Kiwi and Banana 2 teaspoons creamy unsalted natural peanut butter
LUNCH	Tropical Chia Seed Pudding Very Berry Smoothie	Curried Cauliflower and Chickpeas Mashed Eggplant with Garlic	½ egg, scrambled Chunky Green Beans with Lemon
DINNER	Chicken and Sweet Potato Stew Chunky Carrots and Broccoli with Ginger ¼ cup cooked pasta	Lemon-Parsley Salmon Mashed Roasted Zucchini with Thyme ¼ cup cooked pasta	Chicken and Sweet Potato Stew ¼ cup mashed avocado

WEEK 4	MONDAY	TUESDAY	WEDNESDAY
BREAKFAST	Tropical Chia Seed Pudding Baked Apples and Pears	Multigrain Cereal Mashed Kiwi and Banana	Baby's First Pumpkin Pie ¼ cup plain whole-milk yogurt 2 teaspoons creamy unsalted natural peanut butter
LUNCH	Butternut Squash and Lentil Stew Mashed Eggplant with Garlic ¼ cup cooked pasta	Mashed Potatoes with Bell Pepper and Sardines ¼ cup mashed avocado	Root Veggie Beef Stew Chunky Green Beans with Lemon
DINNER	Chicken and Sweet Potato Stew Chunky Green Beans with Lemon	½ egg, scrambled Guacamole with Peas and Cilantro	Lemon-Parsley Salmon Mashed Roasted Zucchini with Thyme ¼ cup cooked pasta

THURSDAY	FRIDAY	SATURDAY	SUNDAY
Tropical Chia Seed Pudding Very Berry Smoothie	Multigrain Cereal Baked Apples and Pears 2 teaspoons creamy unsalted natural peanut butter	Cherry Almond Smoothie ¼ cup plain whole-milk yogurt	Multigrain Cereal Cherry Almond Smoothie
Root Veggie Beef Stew Mashed Sweet Potatoes and Banana	Mashed Potatoes with Bell Pepper and Sardines ¼ cup mashed avocado	Lemon-Parsley Salmon Creamed Spinach with White Beans	Creamed Spinach with White Beans Chunky Green Beans with Lemon
Butternut Squash and Lentil Stew ¼ cup plain whole-milk yogurt ¼ cup cooked pasta	Chicken and Sweet Potato Stew Chunky Green Beans with Lemon	½ egg, scrambled Guacamole with Peas and Cilantro ¼ cup cooked pasta	Root Veggie and Beef Stew Mashed Sweet Potatoes and Banana

THURSDAY	FRIDAY	SATURDAY	SUNDAY
Multigrain Cereal Cherry Almond Smoothie	Mashed Kiwi and Banana ¼ cup plain whole-milk yogurt	Mashed Sweet Potatoes and Banana ½ egg, scrambled	Multigrain Cereal Very Berry Smoothie 2 teaspoons creamy unsalted natural peanut butter
Guacamole with Peas and Cilantro Creamed Spinach with White Beans	Multigrain Cereal Chunky Carrots and Broccoli with Ginger	Creamed Spinach with White Beans Chunky Green Beans with Lemon ¼ cup cooked pasta	Root Veggie Beef Stew Mashed Sweet Potatoes and Banana
Chicken and Sweet Potato Stew Mashed Eggplant with Garlic	Mashed Potatoes with Bell Pepper and Sardines ¼ cup mashed avocado	Root Veggie Beef Stew Mashed Roasted Zucchini with Thyme	Curried Cauliflower and Chickpeas Mashed Roasted Zucchini with Thyme

SHOPPING LIST

PRODUCE

- Apples, 4 medium (about 1½ pounds)
- Avocados, 6 medium (about 3 pounds)
- Bananas, 7 medium (about 2½ pounds)
- Bell pepper, any color, 1 medium (about ¼ to ½ pound)
- Berries, fresh or frozen assorted, 6 cups (about 2 to 3 pounds)
- Broccoli, 1 medium head (about 1 pound)
- Butternut squash, 1 medium (about 2 pounds)
- Carrots, 5 medium (about 1 pound)
- Cauliflower, 1 medium head (about 1½ pounds)
- Cherries, fresh or frozen, 4 cups (about 1½ pounds)
- Cilantro, fresh, 1 bunch
- Eggplant, 2 medium (about 2 to 3 pounds)
- Garlic, fresh, 1 head
- Ginger, fresh, 1-inch piece
- Green beans, 2 pounds
- Kiwi, 6 (about 1 pound)
- Lemons, 2
- Lime, 1
- Onions, 2
- Parsley, fresh, 1 bunch
- Pears, 4 medium (about 1½ pounds)
- Potatoes, Russet or Yukon Gold, 1 pound
- Pumpkin, sugar, 1 medium (4 to 6 pounds)
- Root vegetables, assorted, 1 pound
- Sweet potatoes, 4 medium (about 2 pounds)
- Zucchini, 5 medium (1½ pounds)

MEAT

- Beef, stew meat, 1½ pounds
- Chicken, boneless, skinless thighs, 1½ pounds
- Salmon, boneless fillets, 1½ pounds

DAIRY AND EGGS

- Butter, 2 tablespoons
- Eggs, 1 dozen large
- Yogurt, plain whole milk, 2 cups

FROZEN FOODS

- Green peas, frozen, 1 (13-ounce) bag
- Spinach, frozen chopped, 2 (10-ounce) bags

CANNED AND BOTTLED ITEMS

- Chickpeas, low-sodium, 1 (15.5-ounce) can
- Coconut milk, unsweetened, 1 (13.5-ounce) can
- Great northern or cannellini beans, low-sodium, 1 (15-ounce) can
- Sardines, low-sodium, unsmoked, packed in water or olive oil, 3 (4.4-ounce) cans

PANTRY ITEMS

- Almond butter, creamy unsalted, 1 cup
- Barley, ⅓ cup
- Chia seeds, ¼ cup
- Lentils, red, green, or brown, 1 cup
- Oats, old-fashioned rolled, ⅓ cup
- Oil, olive
- Pasta, small "pastina" shapes like orzo or stars, 1 (13-ounce) box
- Peanut butter, creamy, unsalted, natural, ⅓ cup
- Quinoa, ⅓ cup

SPICES

- Cinnamon, ground
- Cloves, ground
- Cumin, ground
- Curry powder, mild
- Garlic powder
- Ginger, ground
- Nutmeg, ground
- Rosemary, dried
- Thyme, dried

MULTIGRAIN CEREAL

Prep time: 5 minutes   **Cook time:** 15 minutes
Makes: 32 (1-ounce) freezer cubes   **Serving size:** ¼ cup (2 cubes)

This multigrain cereal combines the creaminess of oatmeal and barley cereals with whole, cooked quinoa for added texture. These grains contain fiber to help keep your baby full and prevent constipation, which can become an issue as babies eat more solid food. It pairs well with any puréed or mashed fruit, such as Mango Purée (page 42), Mashed Kiwi and Banana (page 76), or Baked Apples and Pears (page 77).

⅓ cup oat flour (see Oatmeal Cereal, page 49)

⅓ cup barley flour (see Barley Cereal, page 50)

⅓ cup quinoa, rinsed

4 cups water

1. In a large saucepan, combine the oat flour, barley flour, quinoa, and 4 cups of water. Bring to a boil over medium heat. Reduce the heat to low and cook, uncovered, for 15 minutes, stirring occasionally, until the cereal is thick and the quinoa is tender. For a thinner consistency, add more water a few tablespoons at a time. For a thicker consistency, continue to cook, stirring frequently.

2. Cool and serve, or transfer to an ice cube tray and freeze. (See page 62 for storage, defrosting, and reheating instructions.)

TIP: For a chunkier texture, use whole oats instead of oat flour. Don't use whole barley because it can be a choking hazard for babies.

BABY'S FIRST PUMPKIN PIE

Prep time: 5 minutes   Cook time: 45 minutes
Makes: 32 (1-ounce) freezer cubes   Serving size: ¼ cup (2 cubes)

You don't have to wait for fall weather to give your baby their first taste of pumpkin pie. Your baby will love the warm, rich flavors any time of year. Cooking a sugar pumpkin is as easy as any other kind of winter squash and gives you that classic pumpkin pie flavor. You could also substitute butternut squash or 2 (15-ounce) cans of pumpkin—simply choose pure, unsweetened pumpkin purée and not pumpkin pie filling.

1 (4- to 6-pound)
  sugar pumpkin
2 teaspoons ground cinnamon
1 teaspoon ground ginger
½ teaspoon ground nutmeg
¼ teaspoon ground cloves

Preheat the oven to 425°F. Line a rimmed baking sheet with parchment paper.

Remove the ends and cut the pumpkin in half lengthwise. Scoop out and discard the seeds. Cut each half of the pumpkin into 2 to 3 large wedges.

Place the pumpkin wedges, cut-side down, on the prepared baking sheet. Bake for 30 to 45 minutes, or until soft.

Remove the pumpkin from the oven and allow to cool slightly. Use a spoon to scoop the pumpkin flesh and place in a bowl. Add the spices and mash with a fork until mostly smooth.

Serve, or transfer to an ice cube tray and freeze. (See page 62 for storage, defrosting, and reheating instructions.)

TIP: Try pairing pumpkin pie with warm Multigrain Cereal (page 70), or with Baked Apples and Pears (page 77) and topped with a spoonful of plain yogurt.

TROPICAL CHIA SEED PUDDING

Prep time: 5 minutes, plus 30 minutes to set
Makes: 16 (1-ounce) freezer cubes · **Serving size:** 2 tablespoons (1 cube)

Chia seeds may be tiny, but they are mighty! They magically absorb any liquid they touch and form a thick gel or pudding. They're also a good source of omega-3 fatty acids, which support your baby's brain development. In this tropical version, creamy coconut milk provides extra calories to fuel your baby's rapid growth. This chia seed pudding isn't naturally sweet, but it pairs well with puréed or mashed fruit, like mango or banana.

FOR THE PUDDING

¼ cup chia seeds
1 (13.5-ounce) can
  unsweetened coconut milk

FOR SERVING

2 tablespoons (1 freezer cube)
  puréed or mashed fruit, like
  banana, mango, or kiwi

TO MAKE THE PUDDING

1. In a small bowl, combine the chia seeds and coconut milk. Stir until combined.

2. Let stand in the refrigerator for 20 to 30 minutes, or until thick.

3. Serve chilled, or refrigerate or freeze.

TO SERVE

4. Combine 2 tablespoons chia seed pudding with 2 tablespoons puréed or mashed fruit.

TIP: Chia seed pudding will thicken further in the freezer, so you may need to thin out each serving with 1 to 2 teaspoons of water after defrosting.

STORAGE: To use within 3 days, store in an airtight container and refrigerate. Or to store for up to 3 months, freeze in ice cube trays. Transfer the frozen cubes to a zip-top bag, label with the recipe name and date, and store. Defrost the frozen chia seed pudding in the refrigerator or in a cold-water bath. Microwaving is not recommended.

VERY BERRY SMOOTHIE

Prep time: 5 minutes
Makes: 32 (1-ounce) freezer cubes   Serving size: ¼ cup (2 cubes)

Your baby will love the sweet-tart flavor and the captivating texture that comes from berries. Customize this recipe using any combination of berries you like. You can serve this smoothie with a thicker food such as Multigrain Cereal (page 70) or Tropical Chia Seed Pudding (page 72), or with plain whole-milk yogurt. You can also let your baby practice drinking this smoothie from an open cup, as it's thicker than plain water and may be easier for them to handle.

6 cups fresh or frozen mixed berries (blueberries, raspberries, strawberries, blackberries)

1 cup water

Add the berries and water to a blender or food processor. Blend until mostly smooth, adding a few tablespoons of water as needed to achieve the desired consistency.

Serve, or transfer to an ice cube tray and freeze. (See page 62 for storage, defrosting, and reheating instructions.)

TIP: Freeze some of this smoothie in 1-ounce popsicle molds for a cool and comforting treat that can help your baby find relief when teething.

CHERRY ALMOND SMOOTHIE

Prep time: 5 minutes
Makes: 32 (1-ounce) freezer cubes   **Serving size:** ¼ cup (2 cubes)

Tree nuts like almonds are a protein-packed source of nutrition for your baby. Even though tree nuts are one of the most common food allergies, delaying their introduction will not prevent an allergy. Smooth nut butters, like almond butter, are a safe way to give your baby tree nuts without the choking hazard of whole or large pieces. Serve with Multigrain Cereal (page 70) or plain whole-milk yogurt.

4 cups fresh or frozen sweet cherries, pitted (about 1½ pounds)

1 cup creamy, unsalted almond butter

1 cup water

1. Add the cherries, almond butter, and water to a blender or food processor. Blend until mostly smooth, adding a few tablespoons of water as needed to achieve the desired consistency.

2. Serve, or transfer to an ice cube tray and freeze. (See page 62 for storage, defrosting, and reheating instructions.)

TIP: Try making your own almond butter by combining 2 cups of dry-roasted unsalted almonds with 1 tablespoon neutral-flavored oil (such as canola or sunflower oil) in a blender or food processor until smooth.

CHUNKY CARROTS AND BROCCOLI WITH GINGER

Prep time: 10 minutes   Cook time: 15 minutes
Makes: 32 (1-ounce) freezer cubes   Serving size: ¼ cup (2 cubes)

Your baby might be a little young to try your stir-fry meal, but you can give them the same flavors in a texture just right for them. Let your baby touch and explore the broccoli while you cook; they will be fascinated by the tiny, bumpy florets. For extra flavor, try adding garlic or a drizzle of sesame oil to the dish. Avoid using soy sauce—even the low-sodium versions are too salty for babies this age.

5 medium carrots, peeled and coarsely chopped (about 1 pound)

1 medium head broccoli, coarsely chopped (about 1 pound)

1 tablespoon ginger, peeled and finely chopped

1 cup water

In a medium saucepan with a steamer basket or insert, bring about 1 inch of water to a simmer. Add the carrots and broccoli. Cover and simmer over low heat for 10 to 15 minutes, or until the carrots and broccoli are soft.

Remove from the heat and transfer the carrots and broccoli to a blender or food processor. Add the ginger. Blend until mostly smooth, adding 1 cup of water (plus more as needed) to achieve the desired consistency.

Cool and serve, or transfer to an ice cube tray and freeze. (See page 62 for storage, defrosting, and reheating instructions.)

TIP: Pair with Root Veggie Beef Stew (page 89), Chicken and Sweet Potato Stew (page 90), or Multigrain Cereal (page 70).

MASHED KIWI AND BANANA

Prep time: 5 minutes
Makes: 32 (1-ounce) freezer cubes   **Serving size:** ¼ cup (2 cubes)

The sweet-and-sour combination of bananas and kiwis will keep your baby coming back for more. Kiwis are an excellent source of vitamin C to support your baby's immune system; one kiwi contains more than 100 percent of your baby's daily vitamin C needs. Choose ripe kiwis that yield slightly when you press them with your thumb. If your kiwis are too hard to mash, steam them for a few minutes until they soften.

6 kiwis, halved and flesh removed with a spoon

3 bananas

1. Combine the kiwis and bananas in a medium bowl. Mash with a fork until mostly smooth.

2. Serve, or transfer to an ice cube tray and freeze. (See page 62 for storage, defrosting, and reheating instructions.)

TIP: For a smoother texture, serve with plain yogurt or any puréed cereal. For a chunkier texture, try serving with Tropical Chia Seed Pudding (page 72).

BAKED APPLES AND PEARS

Prep time: 10 minutes   Cook time: 45 minutes
Makes: 32 (1-ounce) freezer cubes   Serving size: ¼ cup (2 cubes)

You may want to sneak a few bites of this dish, which features the delicious taste and texture of apple pie filling! Try boosting the flavor by adding other warm spices like nutmeg, clove, and ginger. Instead of peeling the fruit, simply score it with a fork and the peels will easily mash after they bake: Apple and pear peels are good sources of fiber and antioxidants but can be tough to eat in big pieces.

4 medium apples (about 1½ pounds)

4 medium pears (about 1½ pounds)

1 teaspoon ground cinnamon

1 tablespoon olive oil

Preheat the oven to 400°F. Line a rimmed baking sheet with parchment paper.

Use a fork to gently score all over the outer peel of the apples and pears. Then core and cut them into 1-inch pieces.

Transfer the apples and pears to the prepared baking sheet. Add the cinnamon and olive oil and toss to coat.

Bake for 30 to 45 minutes, stirring halfway through, or until the apples and pears are soft.

Remove from the oven and let cool slightly. Use a fork to mash the apples and pears until mostly smooth. Remove and discard any large pieces of peel.

Serve, or transfer to an ice cube tray and freeze. (See page 62 for storage, defrosting, and reheating instructions.)

TIP: Serve with Butternut Squash and Lentil Stew (page 85), Multigrain Cereal (page 70), or by itself with a dollop of plain yogurt on top.

GUACAMOLE WITH PEAS AND CILANTRO

Prep time: 10 minutes   Cook time: 10 minutes
Makes: 32 (1-ounce) freezer cubes   Serving size: ¼ cup (2 cubes)

It's not your traditional guacamole, but the green peas add a pop of sweetness and a new and challenging texture for your baby to enjoy. Green peas provide protein and iron to make this a complete meal all on its own. This pairs well with Creamed Spinach with White Beans (page 84), Chicken and Sweet Potato Stew (page 90), or Lemon-Parsley Salmon (page 88).

1 (13-ounce) package frozen green peas

3 ripe avocados (about 1½ pounds), pitted, with flesh removed

¼ cup cilantro leaves, finely chopped

Juice of ½ lime

1. In a medium saucepan with a steamer basket or insert, bring about 1 inch of water to a simmer. Add the peas. Cover and simmer over low heat for 7 to 10 minutes, or until the peas are heated through.

2. Remove the peas and transfer to a medium heat-safe bowl. Let cool slightly, then mash with a fork or potato masher until mostly smooth, adding a few tablespoons of water as needed to achieve the desired consistency. Remove and discard any tough peas that won't mash and any large pieces of pea skin.

3. Add the avocado, cilantro, and lime juice. Continue to mash with a fork until mostly smooth.

4. Serve, refrigerate, or freeze.

TIP: For a smoother texture, blend some of the peas in a blender or food processor until smooth. For a chunkier texture, finely chop the avocado instead of mashing it.

STORAGE: To use within 3 days, store in an airtight container and refrigerate. Or to store for up to 3 months, freeze in ice cube trays. Transfer the frozen cubes to a zip-top bag, label with the recipe name and date, and store. Defrost the frozen guacamole in the refrigerator or in a cold-water bath. Serve cool. Microwaving is not recommended.

MASHED SWEET POTATOES AND BANANA

Prep time: 5 minutes   Cook time: 45 minutes
Makes: 32 (1-ounce) freezer cubes   Serving size: ¼ cup (2 cubes)

I first tasted this dish 10 years ago at a small restaurant down the Jersey Shore and instantly knew it was a combination I'd return to again and again. The earthiness of the sweet potatoes is an unexpected and perfect match for the tropical fruitiness of the bananas. Serve with Baked Apples and Pears (page 77), Creamed Spinach with White Beans (page 84), or Lemon-Parsley Salmon (page 88).

2 medium sweet potatoes
  (about 1 pound)
4 bananas
½ teaspoon ground cinnamon

Preheat the oven to 425°F. Line a rimmed baking sheet with aluminum foil or parchment paper.

Prick the sweet potatoes all over with a fork. Place the sweet potatoes on the prepared baking sheet and bake for about 45 minutes, or until soft.

Remove from the oven and let cool slightly. Use a spoon to scoop the cooked sweet potato flesh into a medium bowl. Add the bananas and cinnamon. Use a fork or potato masher to mash the sweet potato and banana until mostly smooth.

Serve, or transfer to an ice cube tray and freeze. (See page 62 for storage, defrosting, and reheating instructions.)

TIP: For a chunkier texture, finely chop the bananas and sweet potatoes and stir to combine. For a smoother texture, mix in a dollop of plain yogurt or mashed avocado.

MASHED ROASTED ZUCCHINI WITH THYME

Prep time: 10 minutes   Cook time: 20 minutes
Makes: 32 (1-ounce) freezer cubes   Serving size: ¼ cup (2 cubes)

If you've never tried roasted zucchini before, you've been missing out. Roasting this mild summer squash enhances its natural sweetness and creates a nice contrast between the soft inside and the browned, crisp outside. Use any variety of summer squash you like, including green zucchini, yellow squash, UFO-shaped pattypan squash, or pale green tatuma squash. Zucchini peel is edible, but I recommend scoring it with a fork prior to roasting it so the texture is more palatable for your baby.

5 medium zucchini (about 1½ pounds)
1 tablespoon olive oil
1 teaspoon dried thyme

1. Preheat the oven to 425°F. Line a rimmed baking sheet with parchment paper.

2. Use a fork to gently score all over the outer peel of the zucchini. Then cut into ½-inch rounds.

3. Transfer the zucchini rounds to the prepared baking sheet. Add the olive oil and thyme and toss to coat. Arrange the zucchini rounds in a single layer.

4. Bake for 20 minutes, flipping halfway during cooking, or until the zucchini is soft and lightly browned.

5. Remove from the oven and let cool slightly. Use a fork to mash the zucchini until mostly smooth, removing any large pieces of peel.

6. Serve, or transfer to an ice cube tray and freeze. (See page 62 for storage, defrosting, and reheating instructions.)

TIP: For a complete meal, pair roasted zucchini with Lemon-Parsley Salmon (page 88), Curried Cauliflower and Chickpeas (page 83), or Root Veggie Beef Stew (page 89).

CHUNKY GREEN BEANS WITH LEMON

Prep time: 5 minutes   Cook time: 15 minutes
Makes: 32 (1-ounce) freezer cubes   Serving size: ¼ cup (2 cubes)

I tried making my daughter puréed green beans when she was a baby, but through trial and error I learned that green beans are not meant to be smooth. This recipe embraces the natural chunky texture of green beans and accents them with both lemon juice and zest for a bold flavor. Pair green beans with Mashed Potatoes with Bell Pepper and Sardines (page 86), Chicken and Sweet Potato Stew (page 90), or scrambled eggs.

2 pounds green
  beans, trimmed
Juice of ½ lemon (about
  1 tablespoon)
Zest of ½ lemon (about
  1 teaspoon)
½ cup water

In a medium saucepan with a steamer basket or insert, bring about 1 inch of water to a simmer. Add the green beans. Cover and simmer over low heat for 10 to 15 minutes, or until the green beans are soft.

Remove from the heat and transfer the green beans to a blender or food processor. Add the lemon juice and lemon zest. Blend until mostly smooth, adding ½ cup of water (plus more as needed) to achieve the desired consistency.

Cool and serve, or transfer to an ice cube tray and freeze. (See page 62 for storage, defrosting, and reheating instructions.)

TIP: The lemon juice also helps the beans keep their bright green color after cooking. Add a squeeze to any green vegetable you like.

MASHED EGGPLANT WITH GARLIC

Prep time: 10 minutes   Cook time: 40 minutes
Makes: 32 (1-ounce) freezer cubes   Serving size: ¼ cup (2 cubes)

Inspired by the Middle Eastern dip baba ghanoush, this recipe embraces the luxuriously mushy texture of well-cooked eggplant. You'll know it's cooked when the flesh is very soft and the skin has darkened and looks like it's collapsing in on itself. This recipe includes roasted garlic, which bakes alongside the eggplant in its own little pouch and adds a toasty flavor to complement the creamy eggplant.

2 medium eggplants (about
  2 to 3 pounds)
1 tablespoon plus 2 teaspoons
  olive oil, divided
4 garlic cloves, peeled and
  left whole

1. Preheat the oven to 425°F. Line a rimmed baking sheet with parchment paper.

2. Cut the eggplant in half lengthwise. Rub the eggplant halves with 1 tablespoon of olive oil, and place cut-side down on the prepared baking sheet. Bake for 30 to 40 minutes, or until the eggplant is very soft. Remove from the oven and let cool slightly.

3. While the eggplant is cooking, place the garlic cloves and 2 teaspoons of olive oil on a small square of aluminum foil. Fold the aluminum foil around the garlic to create a sealed packet. Bake for 20 to 30 minutes, or until the garlic is soft.

4. Remove from the oven and let cool slightly. Use a spoon to scoop the eggplant flesh out of the skin into a medium bowl. Add the garlic and mash with a fork until mostly smooth.

5. Serve, or transfer to an ice cube tray and freeze. (See page 62 for storage, defrosting, and reheating instructions.)

TIP: Serve with Butternut Squash and Lentil Stew (page 85), Curried Cauliflower and Chickpeas (page 83), or with a dollop of plain yogurt on top.

CURRIED CAULIFLOWER AND CHICKPEAS

Prep time: 5 minutes   Cook time: 10 minutes
Makes: 32 (1-ounce) freezer cubes   Serving size: ¼ cup (2 cubes)

You can absolutely use spices like curry to flavor your baby's food. It's a myth that babies can only handle bland food. In fact, serving lots of different flavors when baby is little can help them grow into an adventurous eater. This dish features iron-rich chickpeas, an essential mineral for healthy blood. If you don't have fresh cauliflower, you can easily substitute with frozen; just heat it thoroughly on the stove or in the microwave.

1 medium head fresh cauliflower, cored and coarsely chopped (about 1½ pounds)

1 (15.5-ounce) can low-sodium chickpeas, drained and rinsed

2 tablespoons olive oil

2 teaspoons mild curry powder

2 tablespoons water

In a medium saucepan with a steamer basket or insert, bring about 1 inch of water to a simmer. Add the cauliflower. Cover and simmer over low heat for 7 to 10 minutes, or until the cauliflower is soft.

In a blender or food processor, add the chickpeas, olive oil, curry powder, and water. Process until smooth.

Add the cooked cauliflower to the chickpea mixture. Blend until mostly smooth, adding a few additional tablespoons of water as needed to achieve the desired consistency.

Cool and serve, or transfer to an ice cube tray and freeze. (See page 62 for storage, defrosting, and reheating instructions.)

TIP: For a smoother texture, serve with plain yogurt or mashed avocado. And for a colorful contrast, serve with Chunky Green Beans with Lemon (page 81).

CREAMED SPINACH WITH WHITE BEANS

Prep time: 5 minutes   Cook time: 10 minutes
Makes: 30 (1-ounce) freezer cubes   Serving size: ¼ cup (2 cubes)

In my house, any recipe that starts with sautéing an onion in olive oil is a guaranteed winner. This one is no exception. And once you mash the white beans with a little water and mix in chopped spinach, you get a thick, rich consistency similar to creamed spinach. You can use fresh spinach in lieu of frozen; just chop it finely before cooking it so it doesn't pose a choking hazard. You'll need about two pounds of fresh leaf spinach to substitute.

1 tablespoon olive oil

1 onion, finely chopped

1 (15-ounce can) low-sodium great northern or cannellini beans, drained and rinsed

½ cup water

½ teaspoon garlic powder

2 (10-ounce) packages frozen chopped spinach, defrosted and squeezed to remove excess water

1. In a medium skillet over medium-low heat, heat the olive oil. Add the onion and cook for 5 to 7 minutes, stirring frequently to prevent browning, until the onion has softened.

2. Add the beans, water, and garlic powder to the skillet. Mash and stir the beans until mostly smooth, adding a few additional tablespoons of water as needed to achieve the desired consistency.

3. Add the spinach to the bean mixture and stir to combine. Cook for 1 to 2 minutes, or until the spinach is heated through.

4. Cool and serve, or transfer to an ice cube tray and freeze. (See page 62 for storage, defrosting, and reheating instructions.)

TIP: Make a complete meal with Lemon-Parsley Salmon (page 88), Chicken and Sweet Potato Stew (page 90), or a scrambled egg.

BUTTERNUT SQUASH AND LENTIL STEW

Prep time: 10 minutes   Cook time: 20 minutes
Makes: 32 (1-ounce) freezer cubes   Serving size: ¼ cup (2 cubes)

If your baby loved butternut squash and lentils separately, they will absolutely love them cooked together in this stew. Cumin adds a subtle smoky-savory flavor that balances out the sweetness of the butternut squash. Really mix it up by also adding garlic powder, onion powder, or paprika. You can also substitute a different type of winter squash, like acorn squash, sugar pumpkin, or my favorite, silky-smooth kabocha squash.

1 cup dried red, green, or brown lentils, picked over and rinsed

1 medium butternut squash (about 2 pounds), peeled, seeds removed, and chopped into 1-inch pieces

1 teaspoon ground cumin

Place the lentils and squash in a medium saucepot and cover with water by several inches. Cover, bring to a simmer, and cook, stirring occasionally, for about 20 minutes, or until the lentils and squash are soft.

Strain the lentils and squash, reserving some of the cooking liquid, and return the mixture to the saucepot. Add the cumin and mash the mixture with a fork or potato masher until mostly smooth, adding a few additional tablespoons of the reserved cooking liquid as needed to achieve the desired consistency.

Cool and serve, or transfer to an ice cube tray and freeze. (See page 62 for storage, defrosting, and reheating instructions.)

TIP: Serve alongside Chunky Green Beans with Lemon (page 81), Baked Apples and Pears (page 77), or Mashed Roasted Zucchini with Thyme (page 80).

MASHED POTATOES WITH BELL PEPPER AND SARDINES

Prep time: 10 minutes   Cook time: 15 minutes
Makes: 32 (1-ounce) freezer cubes   Serving size: ¼ cup (2 cubes)

Sardines are a delicious, low-mercury fish and one of the richest sources of omega-3 fatty acids. They do have a slight fishy flavor, but the sweetness of the potatoes and bell peppers balances it well. Let your baby enjoy all the fiber and iron found in potato skins by scoring the potatoes with a fork instead of peeling them, so they cook up into small, mashable pieces. And don't skimp on the butter! Fats are essential to fuel your baby's growth.

1 pound starchy potatoes (like Russet or Yukon Gold)

1 bell pepper (any color), chopped into bite-size pieces

2 tablespoons butter

3 (4.4-ounce) cans low-sodium unsmoked sardines packed in olive oil or water, drained and bones removed

1. Use a fork to gently score all over the outer skin of the potatoes. Then chop the potatoes into 1-inch pieces.

2. In a medium saucepan with a steamer basket or insert, bring about 1 inch of water to a simmer. Add the potatoes. Cover and simmer over low heat for 10 minutes.

3. Add the bell peppers, cover, and simmer for another 5 minutes, or until the potatoes and peppers are soft.

4. Remove from the heat and transfer the potatoes and peppers to a medium bowl. Add the butter and mash with a fork or potato masher until mostly smooth, adding a few tablespoons of water as needed to achieve the desired consistency. Add the sardines and stir gently to combine.

5. Cool and serve, refrigerate, or freeze.

TIP: Although the tiny bones in sardines are edible (and a great source of calcium) for adults, remove them for your baby, as they can be a choking hazard.

STORAGE: To use within 2 days, store in an airtight container and refrigerate. Or to store for up to 2 months, freeze in ice cube trays. Transfer the frozen cubes to a zip-top bag, label with the recipe name and date, and store. Defrost the frozen mashed potatoes in the refrigerator, in a cold-water bath, or in the microwave. Heat in the microwave in 30-second increments, until heated thoroughly. Allow to cool before serving.

LEMON-PARSLEY SALMON

Prep time: 5 minutes   Cook time: 15 minutes
Makes: 16 (1-ounce) freezer cubes   Serving size: 2 tablespoons (1 cube)

Like sardines, salmon is rich in omega-3 fatty acids. Although wild-caught salmon is more expensive than farmed, it's worth the expense, because wild-caught salmon has a better ratio of fats (more omega-3 and less omega-6) and more than twice the iron of farmed salmon. Create a sealed aluminum foil pouch with juicy lemons inside to keep the fish moist and avoid overcooking.

4 (6-ounce) boneless
  salmon fillets
1 lemon, thinly sliced
¼ cup fresh parsley leaves
  and stems

1. Preheat the oven to 375°F.

2. Line a rimmed baking sheet with aluminum foil. Arrange half of the lemon slices in the center of the foil. Place the salmon fillets on top of the lemon slices. Arrange the parsley and the remaining lemon slices on top of the salmon. Loosely fold the aluminum foil around the salmon, creating a sealed packet.

3. Bake for about 15 minutes, or until the salmon is opaque and registers 145°F with a thermometer.

4. Cool and discard the lemon, parsley, and salmon skin. Use a fork to shred the salmon into small pieces. Serve, refrigerate, or freeze.

TIP: Serve with Butternut Squash and Lentil Stew (page 85), Creamed Spinach with White Beans (page 84), or Mashed Roasted Zucchini with Thyme (page 80).

STORAGE: To use within 2 days, store in an airtight container and refrigerate. Or to store for up to 2 months, freeze in ice cube trays. Transfer the frozen cubes to a zip-top bag, label with the recipe name and date, and store. Defrost the frozen salmon in the refrigerator, in a cold-water bath, or in the microwave. Heat in the microwave in 30-second increments, until heated thoroughly. Allow to cool before serving.

ROOT VEGGIE BEEF STEW

Prep time: 10 minutes   Cook time: 4 to 8 hours in the slow cooker
Makes: 32 (1-ounce) freezer cubes   Serving size: ¼ cup (2 cubes)

Beef is rich in iron, and the kind of iron found in meat is more easily absorbed than the kind found in plant foods. If you don't have a slow cooker, this recipe can be prepared in a heavy pot (like a Dutch oven) on the stove, covered and cooked over low heat for 1 to 1½ hours, until the meat is tender.

1½ pounds stew beef, cut into 1½-inch pieces
1 pound assorted root vegetables (carrots, parsnips, sweet potatoes, turnips, rutabaga), peeled and cut into 1-inch pieces
½ teaspoon dried thyme
½ teaspoon dried rosemary

In a slow cooker, place the beef, vegetables, thyme, and rosemary. Add enough water to halfway cover the vegetables and meat.

Cover and cook on high for 4 hours or low for 8 hours, until the meat is tender and shreds easily with a fork.

Transfer the meat to a bowl, leaving the vegetables and liquid in the slow cooker. Shred the beef into small pieces. Transfer the vegetables and ½ cup of the cooking liquid to the bowl with the meat. Use a fork or potato masher to mash and mix the vegetables with the beef until mostly smooth, adding a few additional tablespoons of cooking liquid as needed to achieve the desired consistency. Reserve the remaining cooking liquid for another use.

Cool and serve, refrigerate, or freeze.

TIP: Use the reserved cooking liquid to add flavor to recipes like Beef Coconut Curry (page 158) or Quinoa Vegetable Stew (page 134).

STORAGE: To use within 2 days, store in an airtight container and refrigerate. Or to store for up to 2 months, freeze in ice cube trays. Transfer the frozen cubes to a zip-top bag, label with the recipe name and date, and store. Defrost the frozen beef stew in the refrigerator, in a cold-water bath, or in the microwave. Heat in the microwave in 30-second increments, until heated thoroughly. Allow to cool before serving.

CHICKEN AND SWEET POTATO STEW

Prep time: 5 minutes   Cook time: 4 to 8 hours in the slow cooker
Makes: 32 (1-ounce) freezer cubes   Serving size: ¼ cup (2 cubes)

The flavor combinations in this chicken stew are truly delightful. As the stew cooks, the sweet potatoes melt into the cooking liquid to create a sweet, creamy sauce for the tender chicken. If you don't have a slow cooker, this recipe can be prepared in a heavy pot on the stove, covered, and cooked over low heat for 30 to 45 minutes, or until the chicken is tender.

2 medium sweet potatoes (about 1 pound), peeled and cut into 1-inch pieces
1½ pounds boneless, skinless chicken thighs
1 small onion, diced
1 teaspoon dried thyme

1. In a slow cooker, place the sweet potatoes, chicken thighs, onion, and thyme. Add enough water to the slow cooker to halfway cover the chicken and sweet potato.

2. Cover and cook on high for 4 hours or low for 8 hours, until the chicken and sweet potatoes are tender and the chicken registers 165°F with a thermometer.

3. Transfer the chicken to a bowl, leaving the sweet potatoes and liquid in the slow cooker. Shred the chicken into small pieces. Transfer the sweet potatoes and ½ cup of the cooking liquid to the bowl with the chicken. Use a fork or potato masher to mash and mix the sweet potatoes with the chicken until mostly smooth, adding a few additional tablespoons of cooking liquid as needed to achieve the desired consistency. Save the reserved cooking liquid for another use.

4. Cool and serve, refrigerate, or freeze.

TIP: Try using the reserved cooking liquid to enhance the flavor of other recipes, such as Chicken with Ratatouille Rice (page 150) or Veggie Turkey Chili (page 148).

STORAGE: To use within 2 days, store in an airtight container and refrigerate. Or to store for up to 2 months, freeze in ice cube trays. Transfer the frozen cubes to a zip-top bag, label with the recipe name and date, and store. Defrost the frozen chicken stew in the refrigerator, in a cold-water bath, or in the microwave. Heat in the microwave in 30-second increments, until heated thoroughly. Allow to cool before serving.

EGG CUPS WITH SPINACH, PEPPERS, AND CHEESE, PAGE 124

Think: Just a few months ago, your baby had never even tasted solid food. And now? They're practically a pro!

The next phase of your baby's culinary journey introduces finger foods—firm yet squishable foods that your baby can pick up using their thumb and forefinger and easily chew. Finger foods help build independence and fine motor skills by letting your baby self-feed.

This chapter features 20 recipes that even grown-ups will enjoy: pancakes, muffins, meatballs, patties, smoothies, and more. You can continue to make these dishes well past your baby's first birthday, serving in larger pieces as your baby matures.

IS YOUR BABY READY FOR STAGE 3?

By the time you get to Stage 3, it may seem like your baby is already starting to take the lead. Many babies will begin to reject mushy foods once they are ready to move on, so if your baby is giving Stage 2 foods a thumbs-down, it may be time for finger foods.

Look for these signs that your baby is ready to start trying Stage 3 foods:

- **Sitting well alone** – Your baby should able to sit well without support.

- **Transferring objects to mouth** – Your baby should bring food to their mouth using their hands.

- **Perfecting their pincer grasp** – Your baby should be practicing their pincer grasp by picking up food and objects with their thumb and forefinger.

- **Chewing skillfully** – Your baby should consistently chew their food with greater skill and ease.

- **Swallowing with mouth closed** – Your baby should start to swallow food with their mouth closed.

- **Moving food side to side** – Your baby should use their tongue to move food from side to side in their mouth.

Remember that even as baby becomes ready for Stage 3 finger foods, you'll still need to avoid foods that pose a choking risk. Serve foods in bite-size pieces—about the size of a pea. Halve or squish naturally round foods, like beans, peas, cherry tomatoes, and blueberries. To serve raw hard fruits and vegetables like apples and carrots, shred them with a grater. Continue to avoid hard candies, whole nuts, raisins, popcorn, and other hard snacks.

GET PREPPED

Many of the recipes in this section are baked in the oven. Make smart use of your time (and keep your utility bill down) by grouping together recipes that bake at the same temperature. Freezer storage lengths can be found on each recipe page.

VERY VEGGIE TOMATO SAUCE, PAGE 115; **SALMON PATTIES**, PAGE 129

RECIPE NAME	PAGE NUMBER	SERVING SIZE	PREP TIME
Baked Falafel with Yogurt Sauce	122	2 falafel patties	15 minutes (after overnight soak)
Green Beans with Almond Butter and Lemon Sauce	119	¼ cup green beans, 1 tablespoon sauce	5 minutes
Peanut Butter Banana Bake	106	½ cup	5 minutes
Teething Biscuits	108	1 biscuit	10 minutes
Mango, Strawberry, Orange, and Yogurt Smoothie	120	½ cup	5 minutes
Avocado, Spinach, Cauliflower, and Banana Smoothie	121	½ cup	5 minutes
Carrot and Prune Muffins	110	1 muffin	15 minutes
Broccoli and Cheese Muffins	114	1 muffin	10 minutes
Very Veggie Tomato Sauce	115	¼ cup	10 minutes
Cinnamon-Roasted Carrots	116	¼ cup	5 minutes
Garlic-Cumin Roasted Sweet Potatoes	117	¼ cup	5 minutes
Egg Cups with Spinach, Peppers, and Cheese	124	1 egg cup	5 minutes
Ginger-Garlic Beef Meatballs	125	2 meatballs	10 minutes
Turkey Meatballs with Onions and Peppers	128	2 meatballs	10 minutes
Salmon Patties	129	2 patties	10 minutes
Ginger-Scallion Poached Chicken	126	1 ounce	5 minutes
Beets with Oranges	118	¼ cup	10 minutes
Chickpea Crackers	112	10 crackers	20 minutes
Parmesan Zucchini Pancakes	111	2 pancakes	10 minutes
Peaches and Cream Baked Oatmeal	107	½ cup	10 minutes

COOK TIME	HOW TO FREEZE	HOW TO THAW
25 minutes	Freeze falafel flat on a baking sheet, then transfer to a zip-top bag once frozen. Do not freeze the sauce.	Reheat from frozen; there is no need to defrost.
15 minutes	Freeze the sauce in ice cube trays filled halfway (1 tablespoon in each cube), then transfer to a zip-top bag once frozen. Do not freeze the green beans.	Defrost in the refrigerator, cold-water bath, or the microwave.
15 minutes	Freeze cut portions in a zip-top bag.	Reheat from frozen; there is no need to defrost.
15 minutes	Freeze in a zip-top bag.	Serve straight from the freezer; there is no need to defrost.
-	Freeze in ice cube trays, then transfer to a zip-top bag once frozen.	Defrost in the refrigerator or a cold-water bath.
-	Freeze in ice cube trays, then transfer to a zip-top bag once frozen.	Defrost in the refrigerator or a cold-water bath.
15 minutes	Freeze in a zip-top bag.	Defrost in the refrigerator or microwave.
15 minutes	Freeze in a zip-top bag.	Defrost in the refrigerator or microwave.
40 minutes	Freeze in ice cube trays, then transfer to a zip-top bag once frozen.	Defrost in the refrigerator, a cold-water bath, or the microwave.
25 minutes	Freeze flat on a baking sheet, then transfer to a zip-top bag once frozen.	Reheat from frozen; there is no need to defrost.
30 minutes	Freeze flat on a baking sheet, then transfer to a zip-top bag once frozen.	Reheat from frozen; there is no need to defrost.
20 minutes	Individually wrap each egg cup in plastic wrap and freeze in a zip-top bag.	Defrost in the refrigerator or in the microwave.
15 minutes	Freeze flat on a baking sheet, then transfer to a zip-top bag once frozen.	Reheat from frozen; there is no need to defrost.
20 minutes	Freeze flat on a baking sheet, then transfer to a zip-top bag once frozen.	Reheat from frozen; there is no need to defrost.
20 minutes	Freeze flat on a baking sheet, then transfer to a zip-top bag once frozen.	Reheat from frozen; there is no need to defrost.
45 minutes	Individually wrap slices of chicken in plastic wrap and freeze in a zip-top bag.	Defrost in the refrigerator, a cold-water bath, or the microwave.
1 hour	Freeze flat in a zip-top bag.	Defrost in the refrigerator or in a cold-water bath.
30 minutes	Freeze in a zip-top bag.	Serve straight from the freezer; there is no need to defrost.
25 minutes	Freeze flat on a baking sheet, then transfer the frozen pancakes to a zip-top bag.	Reheat from frozen; there is no need to defrost.
40 minutes	Freeze cut portions in a zip-top bag.	Defrost in the refrigerator, a cold-water bath, or the microwave.

MEAL PLAN FOR STAGE 3

In addition to the recipes in this section, complete your baby's meals with hardboiled eggs, cooked pasta and quinoa, toasted bread, and your choice of soft or cooked fruit and vegetables cut into bite-size pieces. Make the pasta and quinoa ahead and freeze flat in zip-top bags. Defrost the cooked pasta or quinoa in the refrigerator, a cold-water bath, or the microwave. When your baby is about 12 months old you can also start to add one to two snacks daily in between meals.

SNACK IDEAS

At about 12 months old, start to serve 1 or 2 snacks daily in between meals.

Chickpea Crackers (page 112) or a Teething Biscuit (page 108) with ¼ cup soft fruit or vegetables

1 hardboiled egg, cut into bite-size pieces, with ¼ cup soft fruit or vegetables

½ cup plain whole-milk yogurt or cottage cheese with ¼ cup soft fruit or vegetables

2 tablespoons shredded cheese with ¼ cup soft fruit or vegetables

Carrot and Prune Muffin (page 110)

Broccoli and Cheese Muffin (page 114)

FRUITS AND VEGETABLES

Serve soft or cooked fruit and vegetables cut into bite-size pieces.

Fruits: apples (cooked), bananas, blackberries, blueberries, cherries, grapes, kiwis, mangos, nectarines, oranges, peaches, pears, plums, raspberries, strawberries, watermelon

Vegetables: asparagus (cooked), bell peppers (cooked), broccoli (cooked), butternut squash (cooked), carrots (cooked), cauliflower (cooked), cherry tomatoes, green beans (cooked), green peas (cooked), mixed vegetables (cooked), spinach (cooked and chopped), sweet potatoes (cooked), yellow squash (cooked), zucchini (cooked)

GREEN BEANS WITH ALMOND BUTTER AND LEMON SAUCE, PAGE 119

WEEK 1	MONDAY	TUESDAY	WEDNESDAY	
BREAKFAST	Mango, Strawberry Orange, and Yogurt Smoothie (page 120) ½ slice whole wheat bread, toasted, with butter, and cut into bite-size pieces	Carrot and Prune Muffin (page 110) with 2 teaspoons peanut butter ¼ cup fruit	Peanut Butter Banana Bake (page 106) ½ cup plain whole-milk yogurt	
LUNCH	Garlic-Cumin Roasted Sweet Potatoes (page 117) ¼ cup canned black beans, rinsed and mashed ¼ cup diced avocado ¼ cup fruit	Parmesan Zucchini Pancakes (page 111) Cinnamon-Roasted Carrots (page 116) ¼ cup diced avocado	Egg Cups with Spinach, Peppers, and Cheese (page 124) ½ slice whole wheat bread, toasted, with butter, and cut into bite-size pieces ¼ cup fruit	
DINNER	Salmon Patties (page 129) Very Veggie Tomato Sauce (page 115) ½ cup cooked pasta	Baked Falafel with Yogurt Sauce (page 122) ¼ cup fruit ¼ cup vegetables	Ginger-Scallion Poached Chicken (page 126) Green Beans with Almond Butter and Lemon Sauce (page 119) ½ cup cooked quinoa with mashed avocado	

WEEK 2	MONDAY	TUESDAY	WEDNESDAY	
BREAKFAST	Peanut Butter Banana Bake ¼ cup fruit	Carrot and Prune Muffin ½ cup plain whole-milk yogurt	Egg Cups with Spinach, Peppers, and Cheese ½ cup oatmeal with cinnamon ¼ cup fruit	
LUNCH	Chickpea Crackers (page 112) 1 hardboiled egg, cut into bite-size pieces ¼ cup vegetables ¼ cup fruit	Turkey Meatballs with Onions and Peppers Green Beans with Almond Butter and Lemon Sauce ¼ cup fruit	Garlic-Cumin Roasted Sweet Potatoes ¼ cup canned black beans, rinsed and mashed 2 tablespoons shredded cheese ¼ cup fruit	
DINNER	Salmon Patties Very Veggie Tomato Sauce ½ cup cooked pasta	Ginger-Scallion Poached Chicken Beets with Oranges ½ cup cooked quinoa with mashed avocado	Ginger-Garlic Beef Meatballs ¼ whole wheat pita bread, cut into bite-size pieces ¼ cup vegetables	

THURSDAY	FRIDAY	SATURDAY	SUNDAY
Avocado, Spinach, Cauliflower, and Banana Smoothie (page 121) ½ cup oatmeal with cinnamon	1 hardboiled egg, cut into bite-size pieces ½ slice whole wheat bread, toasted, with butter, and cut into bite-size pieces ¼ cup fruit	Peaches and Cream Baked Oatmeal (page 107) ¼ cup fruit	Peaches and Cream Baked Oatmeal ¼ cup fruit
Broccoli and Cheese Muffin (page 114) ¼ cup fruit	Beets with Oranges (page 118) Chickpea Crackers (page 112) ¼ cup diced avocado ½ cup plain whole-milk yogurt	Baked Falafel with Yogurt Sauce ¼ whole wheat pita bread, cut into bite-size pieces ¼ cup vegetables	Beets with Oranges Chickpea Crackers 1 hardboiled egg, cut into bite-size pieces
Turkey Meatballs with Onions and Peppers (page 128) Very Veggie Tomato Sauce ½ cup cooked pasta	Garlic-Cumin Roasted Sweet Potatoes ¼ cup canned black beans, rinsed and mashed ¼ cup vegetables 2 tablespoons shredded cheese	Salmon Patties Cinnamon-Roasted Carrots ¼ cup fruit	Ginger-Garlic Beef Meatballs (page 125) ½ cup cooked pasta ¼ cup vegetables

THURSDAY	FRIDAY	SATURDAY	SUNDAY
Peaches and Cream Baked Oatmeal ¼ cup fruit	Mango, Strawberry, Orange, and Yogurt Smoothie ½ cup oatmeal with cinnamon	1 hardboiled egg, cut into bite-size pieces ½ slice whole wheat bread, toasted, with butter, and cut into bite-size pieces ¼ cup fruit	Avocado, Spinach, Cauliflower, and Banana Smoothie ½ slice whole wheat bread, toasted, with butter, and cut into bite-size pieces
Salmon Patties Very Veggie Tomato Sauce ½ cup cooked pasta	Beets with Oranges ¼ cup diced avocado ½ cup plain whole-milk yogurt	Ginger-Garlic Beef Meatballs ½ cup cooked pasta ¼ cup vegetables	Broccoli and Cheese Muffin "pizza" spread with 2 tablespoons Very Veggie Tomato Sauce and sprinkled with 2 tablespoons shredded cheese, then toasted ¼ cup fruit
Ginger-Scallion Poached Chicken Parmesan Zucchini Pancakes ¼ cup vegetables	Turkey Meatballs with Onions and Peppers Green Beans with Almond Butter and Lemon Sauce ½ cup cooked quinoa with mashed avocado	Baked Falafel with Yogurt Sauce ¼ cup vegetables ¼ cup fruit	Ginger-Garlic Beef Meatballs Cinnamon-Roasted Carrots ½ cup cooked quinoa with mashed avocado

WEEK 3	MONDAY	TUESDAY	WEDNESDAY
BREAKFAST	Egg Cups with Spinach, Peppers, and Cheese ½ slice whole wheat bread, toasted, with butter, and cut into bite-size pieces ¼ cup fruit	Mango, Strawberry, Orange, and Yogurt Smoothie ½ cup oatmeal with cinnamon	Peanut Butter Banana Bake ½ cup plain whole-milk yogurt ¼ cup fruit
LUNCH	Beets with Oranges ¼ cup diced avocado ½ cup plain whole-milk yogurt	Chickpea Crackers 1 hardboiled egg, cut into bite-size pieces ¼ cup diced avocado ¼ cup fruit	Broccoli and Cheese Muffin ¼ cup fruit ½ cup vegetables
DINNER	Ginger-Scallion Poached Chicken Green Beans with Almond Butter and Lemon Sauce ½ cup cooked pasta	Salmon Patties Garlic-Cumin Roasted Sweet Potatoes ¼ cup vegetables	Turkey Meatballs with Onions and Peppers Very Veggie Tomato Sauce ½ cup cooked pasta

WEEK 4	MONDAY	TUESDAY	WEDNESDAY
BREAKFAST	Mango, Strawberry, Orange, and Yogurt Smoothie Carrot and Prune Muffin	Peanut Butter Banana Bake ¼ cup fruit	1 hardboiled egg, cut into bite-size pieces ½ slice whole wheat bread, toasted, with butter, and cut into bite-size pieces ¼ cup fruit
LUNCH	Ginger-Scallion Poached Chicken Parmesan Zucchini Pancakes ¼ cup vegetables	Beets with Oranges ¼ cup diced avocado ½ cup plain whole-milk yogurt	Avocado, Spinach, Cauliflower, and Banana Smoothie Broccoli and Cheese Muffin
DINNER	Salmon Patties Very Veggie Tomato Sauce ½ cup cooked pasta ¼ cup fruit	Turkey Meatballs with Onions and Peppers Garlic-Cumin Roasted Sweet Potatoes ½ cup cooked quinoa with mashed avocado	Ginger-Scallion Poached Chicken ½ cup cooked pasta ¼ cup vegetables

THURSDAY	FRIDAY	SATURDAY	SUNDAY
½ cup oatmeal with cinnamon and 2 teaspoons peanut butter ¼ cup fruit	Avocado, Spinach, Cauliflower, and Banana Smoothie Carrot and Prune Muffin	Peaches and Cream Baked Oatmeal ¼ cup fruit	Avocado, Spinach, Cauliflower, and Banana Smoothie ½ cup oatmeal with cinnamon
Parmesan Zucchini Pancakes 1 hardboiled egg, cut into bite-size pieces ¼ cup fruit	Ginger Scallion Poached Chicken ½ cup cooked pasta ¼ cup fruit	Broccoli and Cheese Muffin "pizza" spread with 2 tablespoons Very Veggie Tomato Sauce and sprinkled with 2 tablespoons shredded cheese, then toasted ¼ cup fruit	Carrot and Prune Muffin with 2 teaspoons peanut butter ¼ cup fruit
Ginger-Garlic Beef Meatballs ½ cup cooked quinoa with mashed avocado ¼ cup vegetables	Baked Falafel with Yogurt Sauce Cinnamon-Roasted Carrots ¼ cup vegetables, ¼ whole wheat pita, cut into bite-size pieces	Garlic-Cumin Roasted Sweet Potatoes ¼ cup canned black beans, rinsed and mashed 2 tablespoons shredded cheese ¼ cup vegetables	Salmon Patties ½ cup cooked quinoa with mashed avocado ¼ cup vegetables

THURSDAY	FRIDAY	SATURDAY	SUNDAY
Peaches and Cream Baked Oatmeal ¼ cup fruit	Carrot and Prune Muffin with 2 teaspoons peanut butter ¼ cup fruit	Avocado, Spinach, Cauliflower, and Banana Smoothie ½ cup oatmeal with cinnamon	Egg Cups with Spinach, Peppers, and Cheese ½ slice whole wheat bread, toasted, with butter, and cut into bite-size pieces ¼ cup fruit
Baked Falafel with Yogurt Sauce Cinnamon-Roasted Carrots ¼ whole wheat pita, cut into bite-size pieces	Chickpea Crackers 1 hardboiled egg, cut into bite-size pieces ¼ cup diced avocado ¼ cup fruit	Garlic-Cumin Roasted Sweet Potatoes ¼ cup black beans ¼ cup vegetables 2 tablespoons cheese	Ginger-Garlic Beef Meatballs Beets with Oranges ½ cup cooked quinoa with mashed avocado
Ginger-Garlic Beef Meatballs Green Beans with Almond Butter and Lemon Sauce ½ cup cooked quinoa with mashed avocado	Salmon Patties Very Veggie Tomato Sauce ½ cup cooked pasta	Turkey Meatballs with Onions and Peppers ½ cup cooked quinoa with avocado ¼ cup fruit	Baked Falafel with Yogurt Sauce ¼ cup vegetables ¼ cup fruit

SHOPPING LIST

PRODUCE

- Avocados, 5 medium (about 2 pounds)
- Bananas, 7 medium (about 2½ pounds)
- Beets, 3 medium (about 1 pound)
- Bell peppers, 3 medium (about 1 pound)
- Broccoli florets, ½ pound
- Carrots, 8 medium (about 1½ pounds)
- Fruit, assorted (such as bananas, berries, cherries, peaches, kiwis, mangos), 3 to 4 pounds total
- Garlic, fresh, 1 head
- Ginger, fresh, 4-inch piece (about 4 ounces)
- Green beans, ½ pound
- Lemons, 2
- Mangos, 2 medium (about 1 pound)
- Onion, yellow, 2 medium
- Onion, red, 1 medium
- Oranges, seedless, 4 medium (about 1½ pounds)
- Parsley, fresh, 1 bunch
- Peaches, 2 medium (about ¾ pound)
- Scallions, 1 bunch
- Strawberries, 2 cups, about 1 (16-ounce) package
- Sweet potatoes, 5 medium (about 2¼ pounds)
- Vegetables, assorted (such as peas, cherry tomatoes, broccoli, zucchini), 2 to 3 pounds
- Zucchini, 3 medium (about 1¼ pound)

MEAT

- Beef, ground, 1 pound
- Turkey, ground, 1 pound
- Chicken, bone-in, skin-on breast, 2 pounds

DAIRY AND EGGS

- Cheese, cheddar, shredded, 8 ounces
- Cheese, Parmesan, grated, 2 ounces
- Cheese, ricotta, 1 (15-ounce) container
- Eggs, 3 dozen
- Milk, whole, 4½ cups
- Yogurt, plain whole milk, 6 cups

FROZEN FOODS

- Cauliflower, 1 (10-ounce) package
- Fruit purée (from Stage 1 foods), ½ cup
- Spinach, chopped, 1 (12-ounce) package

CANNED AND BOTTLED ITEMS

- Applesauce, unsweetened, 4 ounces, or Applesauce (page 37)
- Chickpeas, low-sodium, 1 (15.5-ounce) can
- Salmon, wild, 1 (14.75-ounce) can
- Tomato paste, 1 (6-ounce) can
- Tomatoes, diced, 1 (28-ounce) can

PANTRY ITEMS

- Almond butter, creamy unsalted, ½ cup
- Baking powder
- Baking soda
- Bread, 100 percent whole wheat, 8 slices
- Breadcrumbs, plain, 2 cups
- Chickpeas, dried, 1 cup
- Nonstick cooking spray
- Oats, old-fashioned rolled, 4½ cups
- Olive oil
- Pasta, 12 ounces
- Peanut butter, creamy unsalted natural, ¾ cup
- Pita, whole wheat, 1 round
- Prunes, pitted, 1 cup
- Quinoa
- Whole wheat flour, 2 cups

SPICES

- Basil, dried
- Black pepper
- Cinnamon, ground
- Cumin, ground
- Garlic powder
- Onion powder
- Oregano, dried
- Parsley, dried
- Thyme, dried
- Vanilla extract

PEANUT BUTTER BANANA BAKE

Prep time: 5 minutes   Cook time: 15 minutes
Makes: 12 (4-ounce) squares   Serving size: ½ cup

This fun breakfast combines two of my daughter's favorite flavors—peanut butter and banana—in a nutritious and satisfying bite. These pancakes are a complete meal, with protein-packed peanut butter and eggs, whole-grain oats, and vitamin-rich bananas. Plus, they're baked in the oven, so no hovering over the stove while your baby tries to climb up your leg. Serve as is, or mix it up with a yogurt or puréed fruit dip.

Nonstick cooking spray

4 ripe bananas

3 large eggs

½ cup creamy unsalted natural peanut butter

1 teaspoon ground cinnamon

⅔ cup old-fashioned rolled or quick oats

1. Preheat the oven to 350°F. Lightly coat a 9-by-13-inch baking dish with nonstick cooking spray.

2. In a large bowl, mash the bananas with a fork or potato masher until mostly smooth. Stir in the eggs, peanut butter, cinnamon, and oats. Mix until fully combined.

3. Pour the mixture into the prepared baking dish, spreading into an even layer. Bake for about 15 minutes, or until completely set.

4. Remove from the oven, allow to cool, and serve. Or cut into squares and refrigerate or freeze to use later. To serve, cut into pieces about the size of a pea for your baby.

TIP: Make this a family-friendly breakfast by cutting the pieces into larger squares for adults and older kids, and serve with fresh fruit and maple syrup.

STORAGE: To use within 3 days, store in an airtight container and refrigerate. Or to store for up to 3 months, freeze cut portions in a zip-top bag labeled with the recipe name and date. Reheat the squares from frozen; there is no need to defrost. Heat in the microwave in 30-second increments, until heated thoroughly. Allow to cool before serving.

PEACHES AND CREAM BAKED OATMEAL

Prep time: 10 minutes   Cook time: 40 minutes
Makes: 12 (½-cup) servings   Serving size: ½ cup

This warm and satisfying breakfast combines hearty oats with juicy, bright peaches. It's impressive enough to make for a fancy weekend brunch and easy enough for a reheat-and-eat weekday breakfast. Use any fresh or frozen summer fruits you like; they'll become soft and juicy as they bake into the oatmeal. Chop larger fruits (such as peaches, plums, and nectarines) before baking to help them break down into bite-size pieces.

Nonstick cooking spray
2 medium peaches, pitted and chopped
2 cups old-fashioned rolled oats
1 teaspoon baking powder
1½ teaspoon ground cinnamon
2 eggs
1½ cups milk
½ cup fruit purée (such as Applesauce, page 37, or Peach Purée, page 39)
2 teaspoons vanilla extract
Plain whole-milk yogurt

Preheat the oven to 375°F. Lightly coat a 9-by-9-inch square baking dish with nonstick cooking spray.

Arrange half of the peaches in an even layer on the bottom of the dish.

In a medium bowl, combine the oats, baking powder, and cinnamon. Add the eggs, milk, fruit purée, and vanilla. Stir until well combined.

Pour the oat mixture into the baking dish. Arrange the remaining peaches on top in an even layer. Bake for 30 to 40 minutes, or until completely set.

Allow to cool and serve. Or cut into squares and refrigerate or freeze to use later. To serve to your baby, cut into pieces about the size of a pea, and add a dollop of yogurt on the side.

TIP: For older kids and adults, drizzle maple syrup on top for some extra sweetness.

STORAGE: To use within 3 days, store in an airtight container and refrigerate. Or to store for up to 3 months, freeze cut into portions in a zip-top bag labeled with the recipe name and date. Defrost the frozen baked oatmeal in the refrigerator or in the microwave. Heat in the microwave in 30-second increments, until heated thoroughly. Allow to cool before serving.

TEETHING BISCUITS

Prep time: 10 minutes   **Cook time:** 15 minutes
Makes: 12 biscuits   **Serving size:** 1 biscuit

Any parent will tell you that teething is tough on the whole family. Babies struggle with the constant pain and discomfort in their mouths, leaving parents feeling helpless. These teething biscuits might just be the dense and gnawable texture your baby needs. Made from a few simple and wholesome ingredients, with no added sugar, these biscuits bake up with a tough texture that safely crumbles once your baby chews off a piece.

¾ cup whole wheat flour

1 egg yolk

2 tablespoons olive oil

¼ cup unsweetened applesauce, or Applesauce (page 37)

¼ teaspoon ground cinnamon

1. Preheat the oven to 350°F.

2. In a small bowl, combine the whole wheat flour, egg yolk, olive oil, applesauce, and cinnamon until thoroughly mixed. The dough should be moderately firm and not sticky. If the dough is too firm, add another 1 to 2 tablespoons of applesauce. If the dough is too soft, add another 1 to 2 tablespoons of flour.

3. Transfer the dough to a sheet of parchment or wax paper, cover with another sheet of paper, and use a rolling pin to roll it into a rectangle about ¼-inch thick. Remove the top sheet of paper and cut the dough into roughly 1-by-4-inch rectangles.

4. Transfer the parchment paper containing the dough onto a baking sheet. Separate the pieces of cut dough so they are not touching, and use your fingers to round the corners of each piece of dough so they don't become sharp after baking.

5. Bake for 10 to 12 minutes, or until the biscuits are dry to the touch and slightly browned along the edges. They will harden further as they cool.

6. Allow to fully cool on a wire rack and serve or store for later.

TIP: You can serve these teething biscuits straight from the freezer. The cold biscuits will soothe your baby's gums and defrost as they chew.

STORAGE: To use within 3 days, store in an airtight container on the counter. Or to store for up to 3 months, freeze in a zip-top bag labeled with the recipe name and date.

CARROT AND PRUNE MUFFINS

Prep time: 15 minutes   Cook time: 15 minutes
Makes: 12 muffins   Serving size: 1 muffin

Cinnamon and apples combine with shredded carrots and chopped prunes to create a warm and naturally sweet muffin without needing additional sugar. In the battle against constipation, these muffins can help provide relief.

Nonstick cooking spray
1 cup pitted prunes
1¾ cups whole wheat flour
1½ teaspoons baking powder
½ teaspoon baking soda
1 teaspoon ground cinnamon
1 cup grated carrots (about 2 medium carrots)
2 eggs
1 teaspoon vanilla extract
½ cup unsweetened applesauce, or Applesauce (page 37)
½ cup whole-milk plain yogurt
⅓ cup olive oil

1. Preheat the oven to 425°F. Prepare a muffin tin with nonstick cooking spray or cupcake liners.

2. In a small heat-safe bowl, soak the prunes in hot water for 10 minutes, or until soft. Drain and finely chop the prunes.

3. In a medium bowl, combine the whole wheat flour, baking powder, baking soda, and cinnamon. Add the carrots and prunes and toss to coat.

4. In a separate bowl, combine the eggs, vanilla, applesauce, yogurt, and olive oil. Pour the egg mixture into the flour mixture and stir until just combined.

5. Fill each muffin cup ⅔ full with the batter. Bake for about 15 minutes, until a toothpick comes out clean.

6. Allow to cool on a wire rack and serve or store to eat later.

TIP: To serve, cut the muffins into bite-size pieces for your baby. For older kids and adults, serve muffins whole or cut in half and spread with peanut butter or jam.

STORAGE: To use within 3 days, store in an airtight container and refrigerate. Or to store for up to 3 months, freeze in zip-top bags labeled with the recipe name and date. Defrost the frozen muffins in the refrigerator or in the microwave. Serve cold or heat in the microwave in 30-second increments, until heated thoroughly. Allow to cool before serving.

PARMESAN ZUCCHINI PANCAKES

Prep time: 10 minutes   Cook time: 25 minutes
Makes: 24 pancakes   Serving size: 2 pancakes

Pancakes are a classic finger food—firm yet soft, and completely delicious. This savory version includes grated zucchini, garlic, onion, and Parmesan cheese. You could also swap out the zucchini for another grated vegetable like sweet potato, carrot, or butternut squash. Cut the pancakes into small pieces to serve for baby, or serve them whole for older kids and adults. Complete your meal with Turkey Meatballs with Onions and Peppers (page 128) and Applesauce (page 37) for dipping.

1 tablespoon olive oil

3 medium zucchini (about 1 pound), grated and squeezed to remove excess liquid

2 eggs

½ teaspoon garlic powder

½ teaspoon onion powder

Freshly ground black pepper

¼ cup grated Parmesan cheese

½ cup whole wheat flour

Preheat the oven to 400°F. Drizzle 1 tablespoon of olive oil onto a rimmed baking sheet.

In a medium bowl, combine the zucchini, eggs, garlic powder, onion powder, black pepper, and Parmesan cheese. Mix until well combined. Add the flour and mix until combined.

For each pancake, spoon 2 tablespoons of pancake mixture onto the prepared baking sheet. Bake for 20 to 25 minutes, flipping halfway, until both sides are golden brown.

Remove from the oven, allow to cool on a wire rack, and serve or store for later.

TIP: Use clean hands or a clean tea towel to thoroughly squeeze out the excess water from the grated zucchini. Too much liquid can leave your pancakes soggy.

STORAGE: To use within 3 days, store in an airtight container and refrigerate. Or to store for up to 3 months, freeze flat on a baking sheet. Transfer the frozen pancakes to a zip-top bag, label with the recipe name and date, and store. Reheat the pancakes from frozen; there is no need to defrost. Place on a baking sheet in a 350°F oven for about 10 minutes, or until heated through. Allow to cool before serving.

CHICKPEA CRACKERS

Prep time: 20 minutes   **Cook time:** 30 minutes
Makes: about 150 crackers   **Serving size:** 10 crackers

Crackers are one my favorite on-the-go snacks, but most are so light they won't satisfy a hungry baby on their own. These crackers are both tasty and filling, with protein-packed chickpeas mixed right into the dough. And with a crispy texture that easily softens as you chew, these crackers are great for older babies to practice chewing without being a choking hazard. If you prefer a softer texture, slightly soften the crackers in warm water or milk before serving.

½ cup low-sodium canned chickpeas, drained, rinsed, and patted dry on a paper towel
1 cup whole wheat flour
2 teaspoons baking powder
4 tablespoons cold butter, cut into cubes
4 to 6 tablespoons cold water

1. Preheat the oven to 400°F. Line a rimmed baking sheet with parchment paper.

2. In a food processor, pulse the chickpeas for about 30 seconds, until they take on a sand-like texture. Add the whole wheat flour and baking powder and pulse once or twice to combine.

3. Add the cold butter and pulse several times, until the butter is well-integrated and the mixture resembles wet sand.

4. With the food processor running, drizzle in the water 1 tablespoon at a time. Stop once the dough starts to pull away from the sides of the food processor.

5. Remove the dough from the food processor and wrap tightly in plastic wrap. Let the dough rest in the refrigerator for 10 minutes.

6. On a lightly floured cutting board, roll out half the dough at a time into a rectangle about ⅛-inch thick. Cut crackers into 1-by-1-inch squares. Use a fork to poke holes in each cracker to allow steam to escape during baking.

Working in batches, transfer the crackers to the prepared baking sheet, leaving a little space in between each cracker. Bake until firm to the touch and brown around the edges, about 10 to 13 minutes. Repeat with the remaining dough.

Allow to cool on a wire rack and serve, or store to use later.

TIP: To serve as a snack or picnic-style meal, top with a thin layer of peanut or almond butter, guacamole, or any leftover puréed or mashed fruit.

STORAGE: To use within 3 days, store in an airtight container on the counter. Or to store for up to 3 months, freeze in zip-top bags labeled with the recipe name and date. There is no need to defrost or reheat the frozen crackers; they can be eaten straight from the freezer or allowed to warm to room temperature for a minute or two. Freezing these crackers doesn't affect the texture at all!

BROCCOLI AND CHEESE MUFFINS

Prep time: 10 minutes   Cook time: 15 minutes
Makes: 12 muffins   Serving size: 1 muffin

These savory muffins are a meal on their own, filled with whole grains, protein, healthy fats, and veggies. As the muffins cook, the broccoli becomes tender and the cheddar cheese melts over the top, forming a crispy outer shell. Serve alongside a Mango, Strawberry, Orange, and Yogurt Smoothie (page 120) or an Avocado, Spinach, Cauliflower, and Banana Smoothie (page 121).

Nonstick cooking spray
1½ cups whole wheat flour
1 teaspoon baking powder
½ teaspoon baking soda
1 teaspoon garlic powder
1 teaspoon onion powder
1½ cups finely chopped broccoli florets (about ½ pound)
1½ cups shredded cheddar cheese, divided
¾ cup milk
½ cup ricotta cheese
2 eggs
⅓ cup olive oil

1. Preheat the oven to 425°F. Prepare a muffin tin with nonstick cooking spray or cupcake liners.

2. In a medium bowl, combine the whole wheat flour, baking powder, baking soda, garlic powder, and onion powder. Add the broccoli and 1 cup of cheddar cheese and toss to coat.

3. In a separate bowl, combine the milk, ricotta cheese, eggs, and olive oil. Pour into the flour mixture and stir until just combined.

4. Fill each muffin cup about ⅔ full with batter. Sprinkle the remaining ½ cup of cheddar cheese on top of the muffins. Bake for about 15 minutes, until a toothpick comes out clean.

5. Allow to cool on a wire rack and serve or store to eat later. To serve to your baby, cut into pieces about the size of a pea.

TIP: For a fun family lunch, try muffin pizzas. Cut the muffins in half, top with tomato sauce and mozzarella cheese, and bake until the cheese is melted.

STORAGE: To use within 3 days, store in an airtight container and refrigerate. Or to store for up to 3 months, freeze in zip-top bags labeled with the recipe name and date. Defrost the frozen muffins in the refrigerator or in the microwave. Serve cold or heat in the microwave in 30-second increments, until heated thoroughly. Allow to cool before serving.

VERY VEGGIE TOMATO SAUCE

Prep time: **15 minutes**   Cook time: **40 minutes**
Makes: **about 5 cups**   Serving size: **¼ cup**

This veggie-packed tomato sauce is so rich and sweet, you might just use it all the time instead of regular tomato sauce. Don't think of it as sneaking extra vegetables—you're showcasing them in an amazing sauce full of flavor and nutrients! Use any combination of vegetables you like, but choosing mostly red, orange, or white vegetables will keep the sauce a bright red color.

3 tablespoons olive oil

1 onion, chopped

4 cloves garlic, chopped

2 tablespoons tomato paste

1 medium carrot, finely chopped

1 bell pepper, chopped

½ medium sweet potato, peeled and chopped

½ cup chopped cauliflower

½ cup frozen spinach

1 teaspoon dried thyme

1 teaspoon dried basil

1 teaspoon dried oregano

1 (28-ounce) can diced tomatoes

Heat the olive oil in a large saucepot over medium heat. Add the onion and cook for 3 to 5 minutes, or until soft. Add the garlic, tomato paste, carrot, bell pepper, sweet potato, cauliflower, spinach, thyme, basil, and oregano. Cook, stirring frequently, for 2 minutes, or until fragrant.

Add the tomatoes with their juices and stir. Reduce the heat to low and simmer, partially covered, for 20 to 30 minutes, or until the sweet potatoes and carrots are soft.

Carefully transfer the sauce to a blender or food processor and blend until smooth, working in batches if necessary. If the sauce is too thick, add ¼ to ½ cup water.

Allow to cool and serve, or store to use later.

TIP: The whole family will love this sauce served with Salmon Patties (page 129) and well-cooked pasta.

STORAGE: To use within 3 days, store in an airtight container and refrigerate. Or to store for up to 3 months, freeze in ice cube trays. Transfer the frozen cubes to a zip-top bag, label with the recipe name and date, and store. Defrost the frozen sauce in the refrigerator, in a cold-water bath, or in the microwave. Heat in the microwave in 30-second increments, until heated thoroughly. Allow to cool before serving.

CINNAMON-ROASTED CARROTS

Prep time: 5 minutes   Cook time: 25 minutes
Makes: 10 (¼-cup) servings   Serving size: ¼ cup

These carrots are such a hit in my house, they're gobbled up faster than I can serve them. Roasting brings out the carrots' natural sweetness and adds a lovely crisp texture. Cinnamon further enhances that sweetness—but for a savory spin, instead of cinnamon, try using one teaspoon each of sweet paprika and dried parsley. Watch the carrots carefully after flipping, as they can burn quickly during those last few minutes in the oven.

5 medium carrots (about 1 pound), peeled and cut into sticks about the width of a pencil

2 tablespoons olive oil

1 teaspoon ground cinnamon

1. Preheat the oven to 425°F.

2. Add the carrots to a rimmed baking sheet. Drizzle the olive oil and sprinkle the cinnamon on top. Toss the carrots to coat.

3. Bake for 20 to 25 minutes, flipping them halfway through, until carrots are soft and golden brown.

4. Allow to cool and serve, or store to eat later. To serve to your baby, cut each carrot stick into pieces about the size of a pea.

TIP: Serve as a side for your next family dinner, or as a snack for your baby, paired with a protein-packed dip like hummus or plain yogurt.

STORAGE: To use within 3 days, store in an airtight container and refrigerate. Or to store for up to 3 months, freeze roasted carrots flat on a baking sheet. Transfer frozen carrots to a zip-top bag, label with the recipe name and date, and store. Reheat the carrots from frozen; there is no need to defrost. Place on a baking sheet in a 350°F oven for about 10 minutes, or until heated through. Allow to cool before serving.

GARLIC-CUMIN ROASTED SWEET POTATOES

Prep time: 5 minutes   Cook time: 30 minutes
Makes: 20 (¼-cup) servings   Serving size: ¼ cup

These roasted sweet potatoes are the perfect sweet-and-savory combination. The natural sweetness of the sweet potato pairs wonderfully with the savory garlic powder and smoky cumin. For even more savory flavor, try adding ½ teaspoon chili powder or smoked paprika. Don't bother peeling the potatoes; the tough skin will pull right off after roasting. Serve whole for older kids and adults, but pull off the skin and cut these potatoes into bite-size pieces for your baby.

2 pounds sweet potatoes
  (3 to 4 medium), sliced
  into ½-inch-thick wedges
2 tablespoons olive oil
1 teaspoon ground cumin
1 teaspoon garlic powder

Preheat the oven to 425°F.

Place the sweet potatoes on a rimmed baking sheet. Drizzle them with the olive oil, sprinkle with the cumin and garlic powder, and toss to coat.

Bake for 25 to 30 minutes, flipping halfway through, or until the sweet potatoes are soft and golden brown.

Allow to cool and serve or store to eat later.

TIP: For a fun family meal, make loaded sweet potato fries by topping them with black beans, diced tomatoes and peppers, and melted cheese.

STORAGE: To use within 3 days, store in an airtight container and refrigerate. Or to store for up to 3 months, freeze roasted sweet potatoes flat on a baking sheet. Transfer frozen sweet potatoes to a zip-top bag, label with the recipe name and date, and store. Reheat the sweet potatoes from frozen; there is no need to defrost. Place on a baking sheet in a 350°F oven for about 10 minutes, or until heated through. Allow to cool before serving.

BEETS WITH ORANGES

Prep time: 10 minutes   Cook time: 1 hour
Makes: 12 (¼-cup) servings   Serving size: ¼ cup

Beets and oranges are one of my favorite flavor combinations. I love how the sweet beets balance out the acidic oranges. Use classic red beets, or, for a different (and less messy!) option, try golden or candy-striped beets, which won't stain. For a side dish the whole family will love, top the beets and oranges with crumbled goat cheese, diced avocado, and a drizzle of olive oil.

3 medium beets (about 1 pound)

3 medium seedless oranges (about 1 pound)

1. Preheat the oven to 400°F.

2. Trim the ends of the beets. Wrap the beets tightly in a large piece of aluminum foil. Bake the beets for 45 minutes to 1 hour, or until a knife can be inserted into the beet with little resistance. Remove the beets from the oven, open the foil to let steam escape, and allow to cool.

3. Once the beets are cool enough to handle, use your fingers to gently rub and remove the skin; it should slip right off. Cut the beets into pieces about the size of a pea.

4. Peel the oranges and separate the segments. Cut each segment into pieces about the size of a pea.

5. In a medium bowl, or in the container you plan to use for storage, mix the beets and oranges together. Serve or store for use later.

TIP: If your baby's dirty diapers turn a reddish color after eating beets, don't panic! This is normal because of the beets' strong red pigment.

STORAGE: To use within 3 days, store in an airtight container and refrigerate. Or to store for up to 3 months, freeze flat in a zip-top bag labeled with the recipe name and date. Defrost ¼ cup portions of the frozen beets and oranges in the refrigerator or in a cold-water bath. Serve cool. Microwaving is not recommended.

GREEN BEANS WITH ALMOND BUTTER AND LEMON SAUCE

Prep time: 5 minutes   Cook time: 15 minutes

Make: 16 (¼ cup) servings   Serving size: ¼ cup green beans, plus 1 tablespoon sauce

One of my favorite side dishes to make for holidays is steamed green beans tossed with butter, lemon juice, and slivered almonds. This recipe takes those classic flavors and turns them into a baby-friendly dish that's easy and quick to prepare. Make a large batch of the sauce, freeze it in portions, and when you're ready to serve, simply heat fresh or frozen green beans and toss with the sauce or serve as a dip.

½ cup creamy unsalted almond butter

¼ cup lemon juice

¼ cup olive oil

4 cups fresh or frozen green beans

In a small bowl, combine the almond butter, lemon juice, and olive oil. Set aside, or refrigerate or freeze the sauce to use later.

In a medium saucepan with a steamer basket or insert, bring about 1 inch of water to a simmer. Add the green beans. Cover and simmer over low heat for 10 to 15 minutes, until the green beans are soft.

Allow the green beans to cool slightly and cut into pieces about the size of a pea. Toss ¼ cup green beans with 1 tablespoon of the sauce, or serve the sauce on the side as a dip.

TIP: Try the sauce with other cooked vegetables, such as cauliflower, carrots, beets, or asparagus. Cut all cooked vegetables into pieces about the size of a pea for your baby.

STORAGE: To use within 3 days, store in an airtight container and refrigerate. Or to store for up to 3 months, freeze the sauce in ice cube trays filled halfway (1 tablespoon in each cube). Transfer the frozen cubes to a zip-top bag, label with the recipe name and date, and store. Defrost the frozen sauce in the refrigerator, in a cold-water bath, or in the microwave. Serve cold or heat in the microwave in 30-second increments. Allow to cool before serving.

MANGO, STRAWBERRY, ORANGE, AND YOGURT SMOOTHIE

Prep time: 5 minutes
Makes: 4 cups   Serving size: ½ cup

Like a sunrise in a glass, this bright and fruity smoothie will instantly bring a smile to your baby's face. I love the combination of sweet mango, bright strawberry, and acidic orange, but you really can't go wrong with any combination of your family's favorite fruits. Plus, smoothies are an excellent way to use up any leftover puréed or mashed foods from Stage 1 and Stage 2, freeing up precious freezer space for more delicious meals.

2 cups fresh or frozen mango chunks (or 8 freezer cubes frozen Mango Purée, page 42)

2 cups fresh or frozen strawberries

1 medium seedless orange, peeled

1 cup plain whole-milk yogurt

½ cup whole milk (or water)

1. In a blender, combine the mangos, strawberries, orange, yogurt, and milk. Blend until smooth.

2. Serve immediately or store to use later.

TIP: Create your own frozen yogurt melts by using a spoon to drop teaspoon-size "dots" of smoothie onto a parchment-lined baking sheet. Freeze, then transfer the dots to a zip-top bag.

STORAGE: To use within 3 days, store in an airtight container and refrigerate. Or to store for up to 3 months, freeze in ice cube trays. Transfer the frozen cubes to a zip-top bag, label with the recipe name and date, and store. Defrost the frozen smoothie in the refrigerator or in a cold-water bath. Serve cold. Microwaving is not recommended.

AVOCADO, SPINACH, CAULIFLOWER, AND BANANA SMOOTHIE

Prep time: **5 minutes**
Makes: **4 cups**   Serving size: **½ cup**

Don't be scared by the bright green color of this smoothie—it's just as sweet as a fruit smoothie. Use extra-ripe bananas for maximum sweetness. Avocado and frozen cauliflower make this smoothie ultra-creamy and rich, and spinach adds to the beautiful green hue. If older kids or adults in your family are hesitant to try a green smoothie, try serving it as a smoothie bowl topped with fresh sliced fruit, shredded coconut, and granola.

1 ripe avocado, peeled
  and pitted
3 ripe bananas
1 cup frozen cauliflower
  florets (or 4 freezer cubes
  Cauliflower Purée, page 47)
½ cup frozen spinach (or
  1 cup fresh spinach)
1 cup whole milk (or water)

In a blender, combine the avocado, banana, cauliflower, spinach, and milk. Blend until smooth.

Serve immediately or store to use later.

TIP: Plan to freeze some of this smoothie in popsicle molds for a perfect summer treat, or to help your baby find relief from teething pains.

STORAGE: To use within 3 days, store in an airtight container and refrigerate. Or to store for up to 3 months, freeze in ice cube trays. Transfer the frozen cubes to a zip-top bag, label with the recipe name and date, and store. Defrost the frozen smoothie in the refrigerator or in a cold-water bath. Serve cold. Microwaving is not recommended.

BAKED FALAFEL WITH YOGURT SAUCE

Prep time: 15 minutes (after overnight soaking)   Cook time: 25 minutes
Makes: 16 falafel patties   Serving size: 2 falafel patties

These falafel are crispy, light, and full of classic Middle Eastern flavors like parsley, cumin, and garlic. Baking the falafel patties on parchment paper drizzled with olive oil gives them that classic crisp texture without all the oil from frying. It may seem like an extra step to use dried chickpeas instead of canned, but it's worth it, because it helps the falafel stay light and airy.

FOR THE FALAFEL

1 cup dried chickpeas, picked over

2 tablespoons olive oil

½ medium red onion

2 garlic cloves, peeled

1 cup fresh parsley leaves

2 teaspoons ground cumin

1 teaspoon baking soda

TO MAKE THE FALAFEL

1. Soak the chickpeas overnight in several inches of water in a covered bowl or storage container. The chickpeas will absorb some of the water and expand as they soak.

2. Preheat the oven to 400°F. Drizzle a rimmed baking sheet with the olive oil.

3. Drain the soaked chickpeas and dry them on a paper towel.

4. In a food processor, combine the chickpeas, red onion, garlic, parsley, cumin, and baking soda. Blend until a coarse paste forms.

5. Form 1½-inch balls of the chickpea mixture and arrange on the prepared baking sheet. Gently press down on each ball to form a patty.

6. Bake for 20 to 25 minutes, flipping halfway through, until golden brown on both sides. Remove from the oven, allow to cool, and serve or store to eat later.

7. To serve to your baby, cut into pieces about the size of a pea.

½ cup plain
  whole-milk yogurt
1 tablespoon lemon juice
1 clove garlic, peeled
  and minced
2 tablespoons fresh parsley,
  finely chopped

To prepare the sauce, in a small bowl, combine the yogurt, lemon juice, garlic, and parsley. Refrigerate for up to 3 days, until ready to serve.

TIP: Turn these falafel into your next family dinner by serving with pita bread, chopped tomatoes and cucumber (grated for baby), hummus, and hot sauce if desired.

STORAGE: To use within 3 days, store in an airtight container and refrigerate. Or to store for up to 3 months, freeze flat on a baking sheet. Transfer the frozen falafel to a zip-top bag, label with the recipe name and date, and store. Do not freeze the sauce. Reheat the falafel from frozen: there is no need to defrost. Place on a baking sheet in a 350°F oven until heated thoroughly, about 10 minutes. Allow to cool before serving.

EGG CUPS WITH SPINACH, PEPPERS, AND CHEESE

Prep time: 5 minutes   Cook time: 20 minutes
Makes: 12 egg cups   Serving size: 1 egg cup

Memorize the basics of this simple egg cup recipe and you'll be able to whip up endless variations without breaking a sweat. I love the combination of sweet bell peppers, spinach, and cheddar cheese, but you can use any vegetables and cheese you like. If you're using very firm vegetables (like carrots or kale), cook them first until tender. For a more grown-up version, try adding cooked sweet potato, cooked crumbled chorizo sausage, and black beans.

Nonstick cooking spray
6 eggs
2 tablespoons milk
Freshly ground black pepper
½ cup diced bell pepper
   (about ½ medium pepper)
½ cup frozen chopped
   spinach, defrosted and
   squeezed to remove
   excess water
½ cup shredded
   cheddar cheese

1. Preheat the oven to 375°F. Coat a muffin tin with nonstick cooking spray or cupcake liners.

2. In a medium bowl, beat the eggs with the milk and black pepper.

3. Divide the bell pepper, spinach, and shredded cheese evenly among the 12 muffin cups. Pour the egg mixture evenly into the muffin cups. Bake for 15 to 20 minutes, or until the egg cups are fully set.

4. Allow to cool and serve or store to eat later. To serve to your baby, cut into pieces about the size of a pea.

TIP: Squeeze as much moisture out of the spinach (or any other cooked leafy greens you choose) as you can. Too much liquid leaves these egg cups soggy.

STORAGE: To use within 3 days, store in an airtight container and refrigerate. Or to store for up to 3 months, freeze individual egg cups tightly wrapped in plastic wrap and stored in a zip-top bag labeled with the recipe name and date. Defrost the frozen egg cups in the refrigerator or in the microwave. Unwrap and heat in the microwave in 30-second increments, until heated thoroughly. Allow to cool before serving.

GINGER-GARLIC BEEF MEATBALLS

Prep time: 10 minutes   Cook time: 15 minutes
Makes: 24 meatballs   Serving size: 2 meatballs

In this recipe, basic beef meatballs get a flavorful, Chinese-inspired update with loads of ginger, garlic, and scallions. Adding egg and milk to the ground beef helps keep these meatballs firm yet moist: the perfect texture for finger foods. Be sure to finely chop the aromatics so your baby doesn't bite into a big chunk of ginger. You could also use the small holes of a grater to make quick work of mincing the ginger and garlic.

1 pound ground beef

2 tablespoons ginger (about a 2-inch piece), minced

4 garlic cloves, minced

2 scallions, white and light green parts, finely chopped

1 egg

½ cup plain breadcrumbs

¼ cup milk

Preheat the oven to 400°F. Line a rimmed baking sheet with parchment paper for easy cleanup.

In a medium bowl, combine the ground beef, ginger, garlic, scallions, egg, breadcrumbs, and milk. Mix until just combined.

Form into 1½-inch balls and arrange on the prepared baking sheet. Bake for about 15 minutes, or until the meatballs register 165°F with a thermometer.

Allow to cool and serve or store to use later. To serve to your baby, cut the meatballs into pieces about the size of a pea.

TIP: To make this a family meal, serve with soft-cooked rice noodles and steamed vegetables (chopped for baby), and with low-sodium soy sauce for adults and older kids.

STORAGE: To use within 3 days, store in an airtight container and refrigerate. Or to store for up to 3 months, freeze on a baking sheet. Transfer the frozen meatballs to a zip-top bag, label with the recipe name and date, and store. Reheat the meatballs from frozen; there is no need to defrost. Heat in the microwave in 30-second increments, until heated thoroughly. Allow to cool before serving.

GINGER-SCALLION POACHED CHICKEN

Prep time: 5 minutes   Cook time: 45 minutes
Makes: 4 cups or 20 (1-ounce) servings   Serving size: about ¼ cup

Although it seems to have fallen out of style, poaching is one of the simplest ways to get tender and juicy chicken. Cook the chicken with the bone and skin on to keep it moist, and don't skimp on the ginger and scallions. Use a thermometer and remove the chicken from the poaching liquid when it registers 160°F. The chicken will continue to cook as it rests, giving you perfectly cooked 165°F meat.

2 bone-in, skin-on chicken
  breasts (about 2 pounds)
2 scallions, trimmed
1 (2-inch) piece ginger, peeled
  and thinly sliced

1. In a large saucepot, place the chicken, scallions, and ginger. Cover with cool water.

2. Heat the pot over medium heat until barely simmering. Reduce the heat to low to maintain a simmer. Partially cover and cook for 30 to 45 minutes, or until the chicken registers 160°F when a thermometer is inserted into the thickest part of the breast.

3. Transfer the chicken from the cooking liquid to a plate and allow to cool, saving the cooking liquid for another use. When the chicken is cool enough to handle, peel off the skin and bones, and cut the meat into ½-inch slices (about 1 ounce per slice).

4. Serve or store to use later. To serve to your baby, cut into pieces about the size of a pea.

TIP: Serve with your choice of steamed vegetables cut into bite-size pieces, and the sauce from Sesame Peanut Noodles with Edamame (page 140) for dipping.

STORAGE: To use within 3 days, store in an airtight container and refrigerate. Or to store for up to 3 months, freeze sliced chicken flat on a baking sheet or wrap individual slices in plastic wrap. Transfer frozen chicken slices to a zip-top bag, label with the recipe name and date, and store. Defrost the frozen chicken in the refrigerator, in a cold-water bath, or in the microwave. Serve cold or heat in the microwave in 30-second increments, until heated thoroughly. Allow to cool before serving.

TURKEY MEATBALLS WITH ONIONS AND PEPPERS

Prep time: **10 minutes** Cook time: **20 minutes**
Makes: **24 meatballs** Serving size: **2 meatballs**

These meatballs are a real treat, with bell peppers adding a subtle sweetness your baby will love. As your baby gets older, cut the meatballs into larger pieces, until one day, before you know it, your child will be able to cut their meatballs all by themselves.

1 tablespoon olive oil
½ onion, finely chopped
1 bell pepper, finely chopped
1 pound ground turkey
1 teaspoon dried thyme
Freshly ground black pepper
1 egg
½ cup plain breadcrumbs
¼ cup milk

1. Preheat the oven to 400°F. Line a rimmed baking sheet with parchment paper.

2. In a skillet over medium heat, heat the olive oil. Add the onion and bell pepper and cook for 3 to 5 minutes, or until the vegetables have slightly softened. Transfer to a medium bowl and allow to cool slightly.

3. Add the ground turkey, thyme, black pepper, egg, breadcrumbs, and milk to the bowl and mix until just combined.

4. Form into 1½-inch balls and arrange on the prepared baking sheet. Bake for about 15 minutes, or until the meatballs register 165°F with a thermometer.

5. Allow to cool and serve or store to use later.

TIP: For a family dinner everyone will love, serve with pasta, Very Veggie Tomato Sauce (page 115), and Parmesan cheese sprinkled on top.

STORAGE: To use within 3 days, store in an airtight container and refrigerate. Or to store for up to 3 months, freeze on a baking sheet. Transfer the frozen meatballs to a zip-top bag, label with the recipe name and date, and store. Reheat the meatballs from frozen; there is no need to defrost. Heat in the microwave in 30-second increments, or on the stove in a pot with tomato sauce for about 10 minutes, or until heated thoroughly. Allow to cool before serving.

SALMON PATTIES

Prep time: 10 minutes   Cook time: 20 minutes
Makes: 24 patties   Serving size: 2 patties

This is an adaptation of my mom's recipe. They're not hard to make, but with a mom's touch, these salmon patties always taste special and full of love. Serve these with pasta, tomato sauce (try Very Veggie Tomato Sauce, page 115), and a side of green peas.

2 tablespoons olive oil

1 (14.75-ounce) can wild salmon, drained and bones removed

½ small onion, finely chopped

1 egg

1 teaspoon dried parsley

Freshly ground black pepper

1 cup plain breadcrumbs, divided

Preheat the oven to 400°F. Drizzle a rimmed baking sheet with the olive oil.

In a medium bowl, combine the salmon, onion, egg, parsley, black pepper, and ½ cup breadcrumbs. Mix to combine.

Spread out the remaining ½ cup breadcrumbs on a plate. Form the salmon mixture into 1-inch balls and press each into the breadcrumbs, flattening the balls into patties, flipping once, to make sure the breadcrumbs adhere to both sides.

Arrange the patties on the prepared baking sheet. Bake for about 20 minutes, flipping halfway through, until both sides are golden brown.

Allow to cool and serve or store to use later. To serve to your baby, cut each patty into pieces about the size of a pea.

TIP: To prepare canned salmon, use your thumbs to gently pull the salmon apart and reveal the bones running down the middle, then peel away the bones.

STORAGE: To use within 3 days, store in an airtight container and refrigerate. Or to store for up to 3 months, freeze flat on a baking sheet. Transfer the frozen patties to a zip-top bag, label with the recipe name and date, and store. Reheat the salmon patties from frozen; there is no need to defrost. Place on a baking sheet in a 350°F oven for about 10 minutes, or until heated thoroughly. Allow to cool before serving. Microwaving is not recommended.

PULLED PORK TACOS WITH MANGO-AVOCADO SALSA, PAGE 146

Goodbye baby, and hello . . . toddler! While parenting a toddler presents its own challenges, with the tools and tips you've learned in this book, feeding doesn't have to be one of them.

Once your child masters the pincer grasp and feeds themselves, your whole family can eat the same meal together. Continue to avoid choking hazards, undercooked meat, poultry, high-mercury fish, and very salty or sugar-sweetened foods. Other than that, there are hardly any restrictions.

In this chapter, you'll find 15 easy dinner recipes the whole family will love, with modifications as needed to make them safe for your toddler.

SPINACH, ASPARAGUS, PEA, AND RICOTTA FRITTATA

Prep time: **10 minutes**   Cook time: **20 minutes**
Yield: **4 servings**   Serving size for toddlers: **⅕ frittata**   Serving size for adults: **¼ frittata**

Breakfast for dinner has never been better than with this veggie-packed cheesy frittata. Use any combination of vegetables you like (totaling 1½ cups), but I love the all-green look with spinach, asparagus, and peas. Avoid a wet frittata by precooking the vegetables so any extra moisture evaporates. After adding the eggs, dollop ricotta cheese all around the pan, creating pockets of cheese that almost act as a sauce when you cut into the frittata.

6 eggs
¼ cup milk
¼ teaspoon salt
Freshly ground black pepper
1 tablespoon butter or olive oil
1 garlic clove, chopped
½ cup frozen green peas
½ cup fresh or frozen asparagus, cut into bite-size pieces
8 ounces fresh spinach, chopped (or ½ cup defrosted frozen spinach, squeezed to remove excess liquid)
½ cup ricotta cheese
2 tablespoons Parmesan cheese

1. Preheat the oven to 425°F.

2. In a medium bowl, whisk the eggs, milk, salt, and black pepper until no streaks of egg white remain.

3. In a cast-iron pan or oven-safe nonstick pan, heat the butter over medium heat. Add the garlic, peas, asparagus, and spinach. Cook for 3 to 5 minutes, or until the vegetables are heated through. Arrange the vegetables evenly throughout the pan.

4. Gently pour the egg mixture over the vegetables. Cook without stirring until the eggs start to set around the sides of the pan, about 2 minutes.

5. Place dollops of the ricotta cheese on top of the eggs, and sprinkle all over with the Parmesan cheese. Transfer to the oven and bake for 8 to 10 minutes, or until the eggs are fully set (the ricotta cheese will be loose).

6. Remove from the oven and cool slightly, then use a flexible spatula to remove the frittata from the pan and transfer onto a cutting board. Serve or store to use later. Cut into wedges for adults and older kids, and into bite-size pieces for your toddler.

TIP: Try breakfast for dinner by serving alongside buttered toast and a bright salad with chopped tomatoes and cucumbers drizzled with olive oil and vinegar.

STORAGE: To use within 3 days, store in an airtight container and refrigerate. Or to store for up to 3 months, freeze individually wrapped wedges of frittata in plastic wrap. Transfer the frozen wrapped frittata wedges to a zip-top bag, label with the recipe name and date, and store. Unwrap and reheat the frittata from frozen; there is no need to defrost. Heat in the microwave in 30-second increments or in a 350°F oven for about 10 minutes, or until heated thoroughly. Cool before serving.

QUINOA VEGETABLE STEW

Prep time: 15 minutes   Cook time: 25 minutes
Makes: 6 cups   Serving size for toddlers: ¾ cup   Serving size for adults: 1½ cups

Quinoa's slightly nutty flavor pairs wonderfully with earthy spices. And because it's high in protein and fiber, this stew will fill you up just as much as a meat- or bean-based stew. Add extra fresh or leftover cooked vegetables such as sweet potato, zucchini, and mushrooms.

2 tablespoons olive oil

1 onion, chopped

1 bell pepper, cut into bite-size pieces

3 cloves garlic, finely chopped

½ teaspoon salt

Freshly ground black pepper

1½ teaspoons ground cumin

1½ teaspoons chili powder

2 tablespoons tomato paste

½ head medium cauliflower, cut into bite-size pieces (about 2 cups)

1 cup quinoa

1 (14.5-ounce) can low-sodium diced tomatoes

4 cups low-sodium vegetable broth (or water)

Fresh chopped cilantro (optional, for garnish)

Diced avocado (optional, for garnish)

1. In a large saucepot or Dutch oven, heat the olive oil over medium heat. Add the onion and bell pepper and cook, stirring occasionally, until the onion begins to soften, about 3 to 5 minutes. Add the garlic, salt, black pepper, cumin, chili powder, and tomato paste. Stir and cook for another minute, until fragrant.

2. Add the cauliflower, quinoa, diced tomatoes with their juices, and broth. Stir to combine. Bring to a boil, then reduce heat to low. Cover and simmer for 20 minutes, or until the quinoa is tender.

3. For thicker stew (optional): Remove 1 cup of the stew and purée in a blender or food processor, then return to the pot and stir (or use a stick blender placed directly in the pot and blend for about 5 seconds).

4. Cool and serve or store for later. Serve with cilantro and avocado, if using.

TIP: For a wary toddler, try adding one of their favorite foods on the side, like cheese, crackers, or fresh fruit.

STORAGE: To use within 3 days, store in an airtight container and refrigerate. Or to store for up to 3 months, freeze flat in a zip-top bag labeled with the recipe name and date. Defrost the frozen stew in the refrigerator, in a cold-water bath, or in the microwave. Heat in a pot on the stove or in the microwave in 1-minute increments, until heated thoroughly. Cool before serving.

CREAMY TOMATO BASIL SOUP WITH LENTILS

Prep time: **10 minutes**   Cook time: **30 minutes**
Makes: **6½ cups**   Serving size for toddlers: **¾ cup**   Serving size for adults: **1½ cups**

This light and creamy tomato soup will transport you right back to childhood. The soup is thickened with lentils rather than cream, giving a boost of fiber, protein, and iron. Use both tomato paste and canned diced tomato for a bright and deep flavor.

1 tablespoon olive oil
1 medium onion, thinly sliced
1 teaspoon salt, divided
Freshly ground black pepper
3 tablespoons tomato paste
1 (28-ounce) can low-sodium
   diced tomatoes
3 cups low-sodium
   vegetable broth
½ cup red lentils, picked over
   and rinsed
½ cup fresh basil leaves,
   kept on the stem

In a large saucepot, heat the olive oil over medium-low heat. Add the onion, ½ teaspoon salt, and black pepper. Cook for 5 to 7 minutes, or until the onions have softened. Add the tomato paste and cook for 1 minute, stirring constantly to avoid burning.

Add the diced tomatoes with their juices, broth, lentils, and whole basil leaves. Stir to combine. Increase the heat to bring to a simmer. Simmer partially covered for about 20 minutes, or until the lentils are soft. Remove the basil leaves and discard.

Carefully transfer the soup to a blender or food processor and blend until smooth, working in batches if necessary.

Cool and serve or store for later.

TIP: Naturally, serve with a grilled cheese sandwich for dipping. You can also add cooked alphabet or star-shaped pasta for maximum nostalgia.

STORAGE: To use within 3 days, store in an airtight container and refrigerate. Or to store for up to 3 months, freeze flat in a zip-top bag labeled with the recipe name and date. Defrost the frozen soup in the refrigerator, in a cold-water bath, or in the microwave. Heat in a pot on the stove or in the microwave in 1-minute increments, until heated thoroughly. Cool before serving.

ROASTED ROOT VEGETABLE AND BARLEY SALAD

Prep time: 15 minutes   Cook time: 35 minutes
Makes: 6 cups   Serving size for toddlers: ¾ cup   Serving size for adults: 1½ cups

Think of this salad as a template with endless variations. Cooked barley has a subtle nutty flavor that pairs nicely with the sweet and earthy root vegetables, the acidic dressing, and the creamy goat cheese. I love to eat this salad warm with the goat cheese melting right into the vegetables, but it's equally delicious served cold. For a heartier meal, add some cooked chicken or shrimp, or a drained and rinsed can of chickpeas.

¼ cup plus 2 tablespoons olive oil, divided

1 cup barley

1½ pounds assorted root vegetables (carrots, parsnips, turnips, beets, rutabaga), peeled and cut into bite-size pieces

½ teaspoon salt, divided

½ teaspoon dried thyme

2 tablespoons finely diced red onion

1½ tablespoons Dijon mustard

3 tablespoons apple cider vinegar

Freshly ground black pepper

4 ounces goat cheese, crumbled

1. Preheat the oven to 425°F. Drizzle a rimmed baking sheet with 2 tablespoons of olive oil.

2. In a medium saucepot, cover the barley with water by several inches. Bring to a boil, then reduce heat, and simmer, uncovered, for about 35 minutes, or until the barley is tender. Drain the barley and transfer to a medium bowl. If you plan to freeze the salad, rinse the barley with cold water to stop the cooking process, then drain.

3. While the barley is cooking, add the root vegetables to the prepared baking sheet. Season with ¼ teaspoon salt and the dried thyme and toss to coat. Bake for 20 to 30 minutes, flipping halfway through, or until the vegetables are soft and golden brown. Remove from the oven and let cool, then transfer to the bowl with the barley. At this point, you can refrigerate or freeze the barley and vegetables to eat later.

4. To prepare the dressing, in a small bowl, whisk together the remaining ¼ cup of olive oil, the red onion, Dijon mustard, apple cider vinegar, the remaining ¼ teaspoon of salt, and black pepper.

5. To serve, toss the dressing with the barley and vegetables, and top with crumbled goat cheese.

TIP: As your toddler gets older, they can help pick out which vegetables to put in the salad, mix the salad, and crumble the goat cheese on top.

STORAGE: To use within 3 days, store in an airtight container and refrigerate. Or to store for up to 3 months, freeze the barley and vegetables flat in a zip-top bag, labeled with the recipe name and date. Do not freeze the dressing or goat cheese. The dressing will keep in the refrigerator for up to 7 days. Defrost the frozen barley and vegetables in the refrigerator, in a cold-water bath, or in the microwave. Serve cold or heat in the microwave in 30-second increments, until heated thoroughly. Allow to cool before serving.

BUTTERNUT SQUASH MAC 'N' CHEESE

Prep time: 10 minutes   Cook time: 50 minutes
Makes: 6 cups   Serving size for toddlers: ¾ cup   Serving size for adults: 1½ cups

This stovetop Butternut Squash Mac 'n' Cheese is so rich and creamy, you won't even think of turning to the boxed version. The roasted butternut squash adds a beautiful orange color and sweetness to contrast the salty cheese. Most mac 'n' cheese recipes use milk and flour to thicken the sauce, but in this recipe, creamy ricotta cheese plays both roles. Ricotta is also low in sodium, making it a great choice for toddlers.

1 medium butternut squash (about 2 pounds)

8 ounces whole wheat elbow macaroni

½ cup ricotta cheese

2 cups shredded cheddar cheese (about 8 ounces)

½ teaspoon yellow mustard

¼ teaspoon garlic powder

¼ teaspoon onion powder

½ teaspoon salt

Freshly ground black pepper

1. Preheat the oven to 425°F. Line a rimmed baking sheet with parchment paper.

2. Remove the ends and cut the butternut squash in half lengthwise. Scoop out and discard the seeds. Place the squash, cut-side down, on the prepared baking sheet. Bake for 30 to 45 minutes, or until soft. Remove from the oven and cool slightly. When the squash is cool enough to handle, use a spoon to scoop out 2 cups of the cooked flesh. Save any remaining cooked squash for another use.

3. While the squash is baking, bring a large pot of water to a boil. Add the macaroni, and cook for 1 to 2 minutes less than the package directs. Reserve 1 cup of the cooking liquid, then drain the macaroni. Leave the macaroni in the colander and set aside while you make the sauce.

4. In the now-empty pot, combine the cooked squash, ricotta cheese, cheddar cheese, mustard, garlic powder, onion powder, salt, and black pepper over medium heat. Stir to combine and bring to a simmer.

5. Return the macaroni to the pot and stir to combine. Add ½ to 1 cup of the reserved cooking liquid to achieve the desired texture. Allow to cool and serve.

TIP: For baked mac 'n' cheese, transfer the pasta mixture to a greased baking dish and top with breadcrumbs and cooked chopped bacon. Bake at 350°F until bubbly, about 15 minutes.

STORAGE: To use within 3 days, store in an airtight container and refrigerate. Or to store for up to 3 months, freeze flat in a zip-top bag labeled with the recipe name and date. Defrost the frozen mac 'n' cheese in the refrigerator, in a cold-water bath, or in the microwave. Heat in a pot on the stove or in the microwave in 1-minute increments, until heated thoroughly. Cool before serving.

SESAME PEANUT NOODLES WITH EDAMAME

Prep time: 15 minutes   Cook time: 15 minutes
Makes: 1 cup sauce; 7 cups noodles   Serving size for toddlers: ¾ cup
Serving size for adults: 1½ cup

This classic takeout dish is incredibly simple to recreate at home. The creamy peanut sauce can be made ahead of time and stored in the refrigerator or freezer, then combined with freshly cooked spaghetti and grated vegetables when it's time to eat. This fully plant-based meal is complete with protein-packed edamame (also known as fresh soybeans), available in the frozen vegetable section of your supermarket. You can also serve this with cooked chicken or shrimp, or diced tofu.

½ cup creamy unsalted natural peanut butter

3 tablespoons unseasoned rice vinegar

2 tablespoons low-sodium soy sauce

1 tablespoon toasted sesame oil

1 clove garlic, finely chopped

1 tablespoon finely chopped ginger

2 tablespoons hot water

8 ounces whole wheat spaghetti

1 cup frozen shelled edamame

1 medium cucumber, seeds removed and grated

1 medium carrot, peeled and grated

1. In a small bowl, combine the peanut butter, rice vinegar, soy sauce, sesame oil, garlic, and ginger. Add the hot water and mix well to combine. If making ahead, store the sauce in the refrigerator or freeze it to use later.

2. When ready to serve, bring a large pot of water to a boil. Cook the spaghetti according to the package directions.

3. About 5 minutes before the spaghetti will finish cooking, add the frozen edamame. Drain the spaghetti and edamame, then rinse with cold water to stop the cooking process. Shake off any excess liquid and return the spaghetti and edamame to the pot. Add the sauce and mix to combine.

4. Serve cool, topped with grated cucumber and carrot. Cut the noodles into bite-size pieces for your toddler.

TIP: The first time you make this dish, try serving your toddler a more familiar version with plain spaghetti, and sauce and vegetables on the side.

STORAGE: To use within 3 days, store in an airtight container and refrigerate. Or to store for up to 3 months, freeze the sauce in ice cube trays. Transfer the frozen cubes to a zip-top bag, label with the recipe name and date, and store. Do not freeze the spaghetti or the grated vegetables. Defrost the frozen sauce in the refrigerator, in a cold-water bath, or in the microwave. Serve cool.

SWEET POTATO AND BLACK BEAN QUESADILLAS

Prep time: 10 minutes   Cook time: 15 minutes
Makes: 2 quesadillas   Serving size for toddlers: ¼ quesadilla   Serving size for adults: ½ quesadilla

When I first made this quesadilla for my daughter, she peeled it apart and carefully inspected the inside before daring to take a bite. She soon fell in love with the sweet and gooey filling, and now devours whole wedges of quesadilla slathered in sour cream and avocado. While cheese is naturally high in sodium, adding sweet potatoes and black beans helps you make a toddler-friendly, low-sodium meal without sacrificing any flavor.

1 cup shredded cheddar or jack cheese

1 cup cooked mashed sweet potato (from about 1 small sweet potato)

1 cup canned low-sodium black beans, drained and rinsed

4 (8-inch) whole wheat or multigrain tortillas

½ cup sour cream

1 avocado, diced

½ cup salsa

1. In a medium bowl, mix together the shredded cheese, sweet potato, and black beans.

2. Heat a large nonstick or cast-iron pan over medium heat. Add one tortilla to the pan and cook for 20 to 30 seconds on each side, until soft and pliable. Spread ½ of the cheese, sweet potato, and black bean mixture in an even layer over the tortilla. Place a second tortilla on top.

3. Press down gently on the tortilla, and cook until the bottom side is light golden brown, about 1 to 2 minutes. Flip the quesadilla and cook until the second side is light golden brown and the filling is hot, another 2 to 3 minutes. Remove from the pan to a cutting board. Repeat with the remaining tortillas and cheese mixture.

4. Cool and serve or store to eat later.

5. When ready to serve, cut into wedges and serve with sour cream, diced avocado, and salsa on the side.

TIP: The first time you make this dish, you may want to serve it to your toddler deconstructed—ingredient presented separately—so they can explore and taste at their own pace.

STORAGE: To use within 3 days, store in an airtight container and refrigerate. Or to store for up to 3 months, freeze the quesadilla whole or in wedges wrapped in plastic wrap. Transfer the frozen quesadillas a zip-top bag, label with the recipe name and date, and store. Unwrap and reheat the quesadillas straight from frozen; there is no need to defrost. Place on a baking sheet in a 350°F oven until heated through, about 10 minutes. Cool before serving. Microwaving is not recommended.

GREEK CHICKEN PITAS

Prep time: 10 minutes | Cook time: 20 minutes
Makes: 8 pita sandwich halves | Serving size for toddlers: ½ pita
Serving size for adults: whole pita

Classic Greek flavors come together in this easy and light meal, perfect for weeknight dinners or summer picnic lunches. Bake the chicken thighs in a flavorful sauce with olive oil, garlic, oregano, and lemon. Then complete your sandwich with fresh tomato, cucumber, red onion, and cheese. For adults and older kids, you could also add marinated olives or artichokes for an extra bite.

FOR THE CHICKEN

2 tablespoons olive oil
2 garlic cloves, finely chopped
Juice of ½ lemon
Zest of ½ lemon
1 teaspoon dried oregano
½ teaspoon salt
Freshly ground black pepper
4 boneless, skinless chicken
  thighs (about 1 pound)

FOR SERVING

4 whole wheat pita breads,
  cut in half
1 medium tomato, chopped
¼ medium red onion,
  thinly sliced
½ medium cucumber,
  finely chopped
4 ounces crumbled
  feta cheese

TO MAKE THE CHICKEN

1. Preheat the oven to 425°F.

2. In a small bowl, combine the olive oil, garlic, lemon juice and zest, oregano, salt, and black pepper.

3. Place the chicken in a 9-by-9-inch baking dish. Pour the sauce over the chicken and toss to coat. Bake for about 20 minutes, or until the chicken registers 165°F with a thermometer. Remove from the oven and cool slightly. Once cool enough to handle, thinly slice the chicken and return it to the baking dish so it can absorb more flavor from the sauce. If making ahead, let the chicken cool and refrigerate or store it to use later.

TO SERVE

4. Make sandwiches for adults and older kids with each pita half stuffed with sliced chicken, tomato, red onion, cucumber, and feta cheese. Serve toddlers a deconstructed sandwich with each item separate on their plate.

TIP: As your toddler gets older, practice naming the color and texture of each ingredient, like crunchy green cucumbers, soft red tomatoes, and chewy brown bread.

STORAGE: To use within 3 days, store in an airtight container and refrigerate. Or to store for up to 3 months, freeze the sliced chicken in a zip-top bag labeled with the recipe name and date. Defrost the frozen chicken in the refrigerator, in a cold-water bath, or in the microwave. Heat in the microwave in 1-minute increments, until heated thoroughly. Cool before serving.

PULLED PORK TACOS WITH MANGO-AVOCADO SALSA

Prep time: 15 minutes   Cook time: 4 to 8 hours in the slow cooker
Makes: 16 tacos   Serving size for toddlers: 1 ounce pork, 1 tortilla, and 2 tablespoons salsa
Serving size for adults: 4 ounces pork, 2 tortillas, and ¼ cup salsa

Taco Tuesday can now be any night of the week! This carnitas-style pulled pork features orange and lime juice along with earthy Mexican spices. If you don't have a slow cooker, this recipe can be prepared in a heavy pot (such as a Dutch oven) on the stove, covered, and cooked over low heat for 2 to 2½ hours, until the meat is tender. Add 2 cups of water before cooking to prevent the meat from drying out.

FOR THE FILLING

3 to 4 pounds boneless pork shoulder, cut into 2-inch pieces
2 teaspoons ground cumin
2 teaspoons ground oregano
1½ teaspoons salt
Freshly ground black pepper
1 medium onion, quartered
2 cloves garlic, roughly chopped
1 cup orange juice
Juice of 1 lime

FOR THE SALSA

2 ripe avocados, chopped into bite-size pieces
1 medium mango, chopped into bite-size pieces
¼ red onion, finely chopped
Juice of 1 lime

FOR SERVING

6-inch corn tortillas (up to 16)

TO MAKE THE FILLING

1. In a slow cooker, place the pork. Sprinkle the cumin, oregano, salt, and black pepper on top, and toss to coat. Add the onion, garlic, orange juice, and lime juice.

2. Cover and cook on high for 4 hours or low for 8 hours, until the pork is tender and the meat registers 160°F with a thermometer. Use a spoon to skim off any large pools of fat, then use two forks to shred the pork. Allow the pork to cool and serve or store it to eat later.

TO MAKE THE SALSA

3. In a medium bowl, combine the avocados, mango, red onion, and lime juice. Gently stir to combine, taking care not to mash the avocados.

TO SERVE

4. Place the desired number of tortillas on a microwave-safe plate and cover with a damp paper towel. Microwave for 30 seconds, until warmed through. Fill each taco with the shredded pork and top with some salsa.

TIP: To take your tacos to the next level, place the shredded pork on an aluminum foil–lined baking sheet and broil for about 5 minutes, or until browned on top.

STORAGE: To use within 3 days, store in an airtight container and refrigerate. Or to store for up to 3 months, freeze the shredded pork flat in a zip-top bag labeled with the recipe name and date. Do not freeze the salsa. Defrost the frozen pork in the refrigerator, in a cold-water bath, or in the microwave. Heat on a baking sheet in a 350°F oven for about 10 minutes, or in the microwave in 1-minute increments, until heated thoroughly. Allow to cool before serving.

VEGGIE TURKEY CHILI

Prep time: 10 minutes   Cook time: 30 minutes
Makes: 7 cups   Serving size for toddlers: ¾ cup   Serving size for adults: 1½ cups

On a rainy day, nothing beats a steaming bowl of chili. This one-pot meal combines iron-rich turkey and beans with smoky spices and lots of vitamin-filled veggies. And, of course, cool and creamy toppings like avocado, cheese, and sour cream take things up a notch. You can also serve this with crackers and hot sauce to adults and older kids. You'll just want to avoid having tortilla chips on the table, because they can be a choking hazard for young children.

FOR THE CHILI

1 tablespoon olive oil

1 medium onion, chopped

3 cloves garlic, chopped

1 medium bell pepper, chopped into bite-size pieces

1 medium zucchini, chopped into bite-size pieces

1 pound ground turkey

2 tablespoons salt-free chili powder

Freshly ground black pepper

1 (15-ounce) can low-sodium pinto beans

1 (14.5-ounce) can low-sodium diced tomatoes

1½ cups low-sodium chicken or vegetable broth (or water)

FOR SERVING

1 avocado, coarsely chopped, divided

1 cup shredded cheddar or jack cheese, divided

½ cup sour cream

Crackers (optional)

Hot sauce (optional)

TO MAKE THE CHILI

1. In a large saucepot or Dutch oven, heat the olive oil over medium-high heat until shimmering. Add the onion, garlic, bell pepper, and zucchini. Cook, stirring occasionally, for 5 minutes, or until the onion has softened slightly. Add the turkey and cook for another 5 minutes, stirring occasionally, until the turkey is no longer pink.

2. Add the chili powder, black pepper, pinto beans with their juices, diced tomatoes with their juices, and broth. Simmer uncovered over medium heat for 20 minutes, stirring occasionally, until the chili has thickened and the vegetables are soft. Adjust the seasoning as needed.

3. Allow the chili to cool and serve or store it to eat later.

TO SERVE

4. Top each bowl of chili with the avocado, cheese, sour cream, and crackers and hot sauce, if using.

Tip: For a picky toddler, reserve ¼ cup of the cooked turkey and vegetables from Step 1. Serve separately on their plate alongside the beans and toppings.

STORAGE: To use within 3 days, store in an airtight container and refrigerate. Or to store for up to 3 months, freeze the chili flat in a zip-top bag labeled with the recipe name and date. Defrost the frozen chili in the refrigerator, in a cold-water bath, or in the microwave. Heat in a pot on the stove or in the microwave in 1-minute increments, until heated thoroughly. Allow it to cool before serving.

CHICKEN WITH RATATOUILLE RICE

Prep time: 15 minutes   Cook time: 45 minutes
Makes: 6 cups   Serving size for toddlers: ¾ cup   Serving size for adults: 1½ cups

This easy, one-pot meal combines all the classic French flavors of ratatouille with juicy chicken and hearty rice. You start by browning the chicken and sautéing the vegetables, then you add the spices, tomatoes, and rice, and slowly cook until all of the flavors meld. For a fussy toddler, avoid mealtime meltdowns by serving one of their favorite fruits or vegetables on the side, to reassure them there's also something they love for dinner.

3 tablespoons olive oil, divided

4 boneless, skinless chicken thighs, cut into 1-inch pieces (about 1 pound)

½ teaspoon salt, divided

Freshly ground black pepper

1 medium onion, chopped

4 cloves garlic, chopped

1 teaspoon dried thyme

1 teaspoon dried parsley

½ medium eggplant, chopped into ½-inch pieces

2 medium zucchini, chopped into ½-inch pieces

1 bell pepper, chopped into ½-inch pieces

¾ cup long-grain white rice

1 (14.5-ounce) can low-sodium diced tomatoes

1 cup low-sodium chicken or vegetable broth (or water)

1. In a large saucepot or Dutch oven, heat 1 tablespoon of olive oil over medium-high heat. Toss the chicken with ¼ teaspoon salt and black pepper, then add to the pot in an even layer. Cook for 3 to 4 minutes, stirring occasionally, or until the chicken has lightly browned on all sides. Transfer the chicken to a plate and set aside.

2. In the same pot, reduce the heat to medium and add the remaining 2 tablespoons of olive oil. Add the onion, garlic, thyme, parsley, remaining ¼ teaspoon salt, and black pepper. Cook, stirring often, for 3 to 5 minutes, or until the onions are translucent. Add the eggplant, zucchini, and bell pepper. Cook for 5 to 7 minutes, stirring often, until the eggplant and zucchini have started to soften.

3. Add the rice, diced tomatoes with their juices, and broth, and stir to combine. Return the chicken to the pot and stir to combine. Reduce heat to low, cover, and cook for about 30 minutes, stirring occasionally, until all of the liquid is absorbed.

4. Allow to cool and serve or store to eat later. To serve to your toddler, cut the chicken into bite-size pieces.

TIP: You can use the remaining half eggplant as an additional vegetable in Quinoa Vegetable Stew (page 134) or Veggie Turkey Chili (page 148).

STORAGE: To use within 3 days, store in an airtight container and refrigerate. Or to store for up to 3 months, freeze flat in a zip-top bag labeled with the recipe name and date. Defrost the frozen ratatouille in the refrigerator, in a cold-water bath, or in the microwave. Heat in the microwave in 1-minute increments, until heated thoroughly. Allow to cool before serving.

MAPLE-MUSTARD SALMON WITH ROASTED VEGETABLES

Prep time: 10 minutes   Cook time: 35 minutes
Yield: 4 adult servings   Serving size for toddlers: ⅓ cup salmon and ½ cup vegetables
Serving size for adults: ¾ cup salmon and 1 cup vegetables

You won't believe how simple this sheet pan recipe is. Start by roasting your favorite hearty vegetables (I love using brussels sprouts, cauliflower, and broccoli) in olive oil, salt, and pepper. Once the vegetables are about halfway cooked, create a space on the pan and nestle the salmon slathered in a sweet and tangy maple-mustard sauce. The salmon and vegetables will finish cooking together, and dinner will be on the table before you know it.

4 cups brussels sprouts, broccoli, or cauliflower (about 1 pound)
2 tablespoons olive oil
½ teaspoon salt
Freshly ground black pepper
2 tablespoons maple syrup
2 tablespoons Dijon mustard
4 (6-ounce) boneless salmon fillets

1. Preheat the oven to 400°F.

2. Prepare the vegetables: halve the brussels sprouts and cut the broccoli or cauliflower into 1-inch pieces.

3. On a rimmed baking sheet, add the vegetables, olive oil, salt, and black pepper, and toss to coat. Bake for 15 to 20 minutes, or until the vegetables have browned on the bottom.

4. While the vegetables are roasting, in a small bowl, combine the maple syrup and Dijon mustard.

5. Remove the vegetables from the oven, flip, and push to either side of the pan to make space for the salmon. Place the salmon skin-side down on the baking sheet. Use a brush or spoon to spread the sauce onto the salmon flesh. Return the baking sheet to the oven and cook for another 10 to 15 minutes, or until the salmon is opaque and registers 145°F with a thermometer.

6. Remove from the oven, allow to cool, and serve or store to eat later. To serve to your toddler, cut the salmon and vegetables into bite-size pieces.

TIP: Give your toddler some choice in which vegetables to make. Toddlers love feeling in charge, and they're more likely to eat a meal they helped to plan.

STORAGE: To use within 3 days, store in an airtight container and refrigerate. Or to store for up to 3 months, freeze the salmon by wrapping it in plastic wrap and placing it in a zip-top bag labeled with the recipe name and date. Freeze the vegetables flat in a zip-top bag labeled with the recipe name and date. Defrost the frozen salmon and vegetables in the refrigerator, in a cold-water bath, or in the microwave. Heat in a 350°F oven for about 10 minutes, or in the microwave in 1-minute increments, until heated thoroughly. Allow to cool before serving.

SHRIMP AND VEGETABLE FRIED RICE

Prep time: 15 minutes   **Cook time:** 20 minutes
Makes: 6 cups   **Serving size for toddlers: ¾ cup**   **Serving size for adults: 1½ cups**

My secret to a good fried rice is to use cold cooked rice, which won't stick to the pan like hot rice will. Rice and other grains are simple to make ahead; just store cooked and cooled grains flat in zip-top bags with 1 or 2 cups in each bag. In a pinch, spread freshly made, hot rice on a rimmed baking sheet to help it to cool off before adding it to the fried rice.

2 tablespoons vegetable oil, divided
1 medium onion, thinly sliced
1 cup chopped fresh or frozen broccoli florets
1 cup frozen mixed vegetables
1 pound peeled and deveined shrimp, patted dry
1 tablespoon finely chopped ginger
2 garlic cloves, chopped
2 scallions, chopped
3 cups cooked rice
2 eggs
2 tablespoons low-sodium soy sauce

1. In a large nonstick skillet, heat 1 tablespoon of vegetable oil over medium-high heat. Add the onion, broccoli, and mixed vegetables. Cook for 3 to 5 minutes, or until the vegetables have slightly softened (if using fresh) or are heated through (if using frozen). Transfer the vegetables to a heat-safe bowl and set aside.

2. In the same pan, add 1 teaspoon of vegetable oil. Add the shrimp and cook for 3 to 4 minutes, flipping at the halfway point, until pink and opaque. Transfer the shrimp to the bowl with the vegetables.

3. In the same pan, add the remaining 2 teaspoons of vegetable oil. Add the ginger, garlic, and scallions. Cook for 30 seconds, or until fragrant. Add the rice and stir to combine. Add the shrimp and vegetable mixture to the rice and stir to combine. Cook, stirring occasionally, until the fried rice is heated through, about 3 to 5 minutes.

4. Make a well in the center of the pan and crack the eggs into the well. Stir the eggs using a wooden spoon or spatula, keeping them in the well, for about 1 minute, until the eggs are halfway cooked. Add the soy sauce and stir to incorporate the eggs into the rice. Stir until everything is combined and the eggs are fully cooked, about 1 minute.

Allow to cool and serve or store to use later. Cut the shrimp and any larger pieces of vegetables into bite-size pieces to serve to your toddler.

TIP: Use any combination of vegetables you like, totaling 2 cups. You can use fresh, frozen, or leftover cooked vegetables.

STORAGE: To use within 3 days, store in an airtight container and refrigerate. Or to store for up to 3 months, freeze flat in a zip-top bag labeled with the recipe name and date. Defrost the frozen fried rice in the refrigerator, in a cold-water bath, or in the microwave. Heat in the microwave in 1-minute increments, until heated thoroughly. Allow to cool before serving.

CRISPY BREADED FISH STICKS WITH YOGURT TARTAR SAUCE

Prep time: 15 minutes   **Cook time:** 20 minutes
Makes: 16 fish sticks   **Serving size for toddlers:** 2 fish sticks
Serving size for adults: 4 fish sticks

I have such fond memories of my mom opening up a box of frozen fish sticks and baking them for a Friday night treat for my family. These homemade fish sticks are nearly as easy as the boxed kind—but far tastier. I love using cod for this recipe because of its meaty, flaky texture and its great nutrition. Cod is one of the few foods high in choline, a nutrient beneficial for your baby's brain development.

FOR THE FISH STICKS

2 tablespoons olive oil

1 egg

1 tablespoon water

½ cup all-purpose flour

1 cup
  unseasoned breadcrumbs

1 pound cod or other
  white-fleshed fish, cut into
  pieces about 2 fingers wide
  (about 1 ounce each)

½ teaspoon salt

½ teaspoon garlic powder

¼ teaspoon onion powder

Freshly ground black pepper

TO MAKE THE FISH STICKS

1. Preheat the oven to 400°F. Drizzle the olive oil onto a rimmed baking sheet.

2. Beat the egg with 1 tablespoon of water.

3. Prepare three shallow bowls: one with the flour, one with the egg mixture, and one with the breadcrumbs.

4. Season the fish with the salt, garlic powder, onion powder, and black pepper. Working one piece at a time, place a piece of fish in the flour, shaking off any excess. Transfer it to the bowl with the egg, fully coating it and letting the excess egg drip off. Then transfer the fish to the bowl with the breadcrumbs, gently pressing so the breadcrumbs adhere. Repeat the process until all the fish pieces are well coated.

5. Arrange the fish on the prepared baking sheet. Bake for 15 to 20 minutes, flipping halfway through, until golden brown on both sides and the fish registers 145°F with a thermometer.

6. Remove from the oven, allow to cool, and serve or store to eat later. Cut into bite-size pieces for your toddler.

½ cup plain full-fat
  Greek yogurt
1 tablespoon lemon juice
2 tablespoons finely chopped
  dill pickle

In a small bowl, combine the yogurt, lemon juice, and pickle. Set aside in the refrigerator for up to 7 days until ready to serve.

TIP: Tartar sauce is a bit of an acquired flavor, so if your toddler isn't quite ready for it, try classic ketchup or ranch dressing for dipping.

STORAGE: To use within 3 days, store in an airtight container and refrigerate. Or to store for up to 3 months, freeze the cooked fish sticks flat in a zip-top bag labeled with the recipe name and date. Do not freeze the sauce. Reheat the fish sticks from frozen; there is no need to defrost. Place on a baking sheet in a 350°F oven for about 10 minutes, or until heated thoroughly. Allow to cool before serving.

BEEF COCONUT CURRY

Prep time: **15 minutes**   Cook time: **4 to 8 hours in the slow cooker**
Makes: **5 cups**   Serving size for toddlers: **¾ cup**   Serving size for adults: **1½ cups**

This warm and comforting beef stew includes the classic Caribbean flavors of curry, sweet potato, fresh ginger, and creamy coconut milk. If you don't have a slow cooker, cook this stew in a heavy pot (like a Dutch oven) on the stovetop, covered, over low heat for 1 to 1½ hours, until the meat is tender. Add 1 cup of water at the start to prevent the meat from drying out.

1 large sweet potato, peeled
   and roughly chopped
1 bell pepper,
   roughly chopped
1½ pounds stew beef, cut into
   2-inch pieces
1 tablespoon flour
1 teaspoon salt
Freshly ground black pepper
2 teaspoons mild
   curry powder
2 tablespoons finely chopped
   ginger (from a 2-inch piece)
1 (13.5-ounce) can
   coconut milk

1. In a slow cooker, place the sweet potato and bell pepper. Add the beef on top. Sprinkle the flour, salt, black pepper, curry powder, and ginger on top of the beef. Pour the coconut milk over the beef and vegetables.

2. Cover and cook on high for 4 hours or low for 8 hours, or until the meat and vegetables are tender and the meat registers 160°F with a thermometer. Use a spoon to skim off any pools of fat, and stir the stew to fully incorporate the coconut milk.

3. Allow to cool and serve or store to use later. To serve to your toddler, cut the meat and vegetables into bite-size pieces.

TIP: Serve with a side of cooked rice and garnish with fresh cilantro if desired. To complete your meal, pair the stew with a fresh salad and tropical fruit.

STORAGE: To use within 3 days, store in an airtight container and refrigerate. Or to store for up to 3 months, freeze flat in a zip-top bag labeled with the recipe name and date. Defrost the frozen stew in the refrigerator, in a cold-water bath, or in the microwave. Heat in a pot on the stove, or in the microwave in 30-second increments, until heated thoroughly. Allow to cool before serving.

CHICKEN WITH RATATOUILLE RICE, PAGE 150

MEASUREMENT CONVERSIONS

Volume Equivalents (Liquid)

US STANDARD	US STANDARD (OUNCES)	METRIC (APPROXIMATE)
2 tablespoons	1 fl. oz.	30 mL
¼ cup	2 fl. oz.	60 mL
½ cup	4 fl. oz.	120 mL
1 cup	8 fl. oz.	240 mL
1½ cups	12 fl. oz.	355 mL
2 cups or 1 pint	16 fl. oz.	475 mL
4 cups or 1 quart	32 fl. oz.	1 L
1 gallon or 4 quarts	128 fl. oz.	4 L

Oven Temperatures

FAHRENHEIT	CELSIUS (APPROXIMATE)
250°F	120°C
300°F	150°C
325°F	165°C
350°F	180°C
375°F	190°C
400°F	200°C
425°F	220°C
450°F	230°C

Volume Equivalents (Dry)

US STANDARD	METRIC (APPROXIMATE)
⅛ teaspoon	0.5 mL
¼ teaspoon	1 mL
½ teaspoon	2 mL
¾ teaspoon	4 mL
1 teaspoon	5 mL
1 tablespoon	15 mL
¼ cup	59 mL
⅓ cup	79 mL
½ cup	118 mL
⅔ cup	156 mL
¾ cup	177 mL
1 cup	235 mL
2 cups or 1 pint	475 mL
3 cups	700 mL
4 cups or 1 quart	1 L

Weight Equivalents

US STANDARD	METRIC (APPROXIMATE)
½ ounce	15 g
1 ounce	30 g
2 ounces	60 g
4 ounces	115 g
8 ounces	225 g
12 ounces	340 g
16 ounces or 1 pound	455 g

RESOURCES

BOOKS

Fearless Feeding: How to Raise Healthy Eaters from High Chair to High School, by Jill Castle and Maryann Jacobsen – Written by two pediatric registered dietitians, this book gives you accurate and practical information for making your own baby food and conquering feeding challenges.

Child of Mine: Feeding with Love and Good Sense, by Ellyn Satter – This child nutrition staple will help you understand not just what to feed your baby but how to help your child become an independent eater who has a healthy relationship with food.

The Big Book of Organic Baby Food, by Stephanie Middleberg, MS, RD, CDN – With more than 230 easy recipes, this book will teach you how to create an endless variety of delicious and healthy meals for your baby.

WEBSITES

WholesomeBabyFood.Momtastic.com – An amazing resource of baby food recipes, plus tips for making and storing homemade baby food and spicing up your baby's meals with creative combinations.

BabyFoode.com – This blog features hundreds of recipes for all stages of baby food, plus toddler and family meals.

HealthyChildren.org (The AAP Parenting Website) – Articles on infant and child health, nutrition, and safety from the American Academy of Pediatrics. This is my go-to site for expert advice.

FoodSafety.gov (Food Safety Blog) – Combining information from government agencies, this website features food safety tips for infants, young children, and families.

ORGANIZATIONS

American Academy of Pediatrics (AAP.org) – This organization of more than 60,000 pediatricians will give you the most accurate information on all things related to your child's health.

Academy of Nutrition and Dietetics (eatright.org/for-kids) – Find articles, family-friendly recipes, and videos to learn how to raise healthy eaters, from registered dietitian nutritionists.

Centers for Disease Control and Prevention (CDC.gov/nutrition) – Learn more about making your own baby food and find the best food safety tips to feed your family safe and healthy food.

REFERENCES

Castle, Jill, and Maryann Jacobsen. *Fearless Feeding: How to Raise Healthy Eaters from High Chair to High School.* San Francisco: Jossey-Bass, 2013.

Chandler, Adam. "Why Americans Lead the World in Food Waste." The Atlantic, July 15, 2016. https://www.theatlantic.com/business /archive/2016/07/american-food-waste/491513

CHOC Children's. "Performing the Heimlich Maneuver on a Child or Infant." YouTube. January 9, 2015: https://www.youtube.com/watch? v=aXaLc-AwX2g

"Choking – Infant Under 1 Year." Medline Plus. Last reviewed January 12, 2019. Accessed December 9, 2019. https://medlineplus.gov/ency/article /000048.htm

"Choking Hazards." Centers for Disease Control and Prevention. Last reviewed May 29, 2019. Accessed November 29, 2019. https://www.cdc.gov /nutrition/infantandtoddlernutrition/foods-and-drinks/choking -hazards.html

"Facts and Statistics." Food Allergy Research & Education. Accessed December 10, 2019. https://www.foodallergy.org/life-with-food-allergies /food-allergy-101/facts-and-statistics

"Four Steps (Clean, Separate, Cook, Chill) to Food Safety." FoodSafety.gov. Last reviewed April 12, 2019. Accessed January 1, 2020. https://www.food safety.gov/keep-food-safe/4-steps-to-food-safety

"Infant Nutrition and Feeding Guide." United States Department of Agriculture. Published April 2019. Accessed November 29, 2019. https://wicworks .fns.usda.gov/resources/infant-nutrition-and-feeding-guide

Jenco, Melissa. "Study 7.6% of Children Have Food Allergies." American Academy of Pediatrics, November 16, 2018. https://www.aappublications .org/news/2018/11/16/foodallergies111618

"Keep Food Safe! Food Safety Basics." United States Department of Agriculture. Last modified December 20, 2016. Accessed January 15, 2020. https://www.fsis.usda.gov/wps/portal/fsis/topics/food-safety-education /get-answers/food-safety-fact-sheets/safe-food-handling/keep-food-safe -food-safety-basics/ct_index

"Magnesium – Health Professional Factsheet." National Institutes of Health. Last updated October 11, 2019. Accessed January 18, 2020. https://ods.od .nih.gov/factsheets/Magnesium-HealthProfessional

"Once Baby Arrives from Food Safety for Moms to Be." U.S. Food & Drug Administration. Last updated April 11, 2019. Accessed January 1, 2020. https://www.fda.gov/food/people-risk-foodborne-illness/once-baby -arrives-food-safety-moms-be

"People at Risk: Children Under Five." FoodSafety.gov. Last reviewed April 26, 2019. Accessed January 1, 2020. https://www.foodsafety.gov /people-at-risk/children-under-five

"Phosphorus – Health Professional Factsheet." National Institutes of Health. Last updated November 21, 2019. Accessed January 18, 2020. https:// ods.od.nih.gov/factsheets/Phosphorus-HealthProfessional

Satter, Ellyn. *Child of Mine: Feeding with Love and Good Sense*. Boulder: Bull Publishing Company, 2000.

"Vitamin A – Health Professional Factsheet." National Institutes of Health. Last updated October 11, 2019. Accessed January 16, 2020. https://ods.od .nih.gov/factsheets/VitaminA-HealthProfessional

"Vitamin C – Health Professional Factsheet." National Institutes of Health. Last updated July 9, 2019. Accessed January 16, 2020. https://ods.od.nih .gov/factsheets/VitaminC-HealthProfessional

"Vitamin D – Health Professional Factsheet." National Institutes of Health. Last updated August 7, 2019. Accessed December 9, 2019. https://ods.od .nih.gov/factsheets/VitaminD-HealthProfessional

INDEX

ACKNOWLEDGMENTS

To my family and friends, thank you for your endless support and encouragement. For Mom, Dad, Pete, Barbara, and Kristin, thank you for always believing in me, and for offering to babysit so I could write and develop recipes. For my husband, Eric, thank you being my biggest fan and partner. And for Ava, thank you for making me a mom, for being my number one taste-tester, and for always giving me your brutally honest feedback.

Thank you to Kayla, my editor, and the entire team at Callisto for your expertise and guidance in bringing this book to life.

And, of course, thanks to all of you who decided to read this book. Your stories, struggles, and successes are the inspiration for this book. I hope that you enjoy making these recipes and serving them to your baby, and that you continue to cook and share meals together for years to come.

ABOUT THE AUTHOR

Stephanie Van't Zelfden, RDN, CDN, is a food and nutrition expert, author, wife, and mom. As a registered dietitian nutritionist, she helps parents learn how to feed their families with confidence and ease.

Stephanie earned a bachelor's degree in Health & Nutrition Science from Brooklyn College, and went on to complete her dietetic internship at Queens College, where she trained in pediatric and family nutrition.

She is the founder and owner of Nutrition Hungry, where she is a nutrition consultant, recipe developer, and blogger. Her writing has appeared in FoodNetwork.com, Healthline, *US News*, *Food & Nutrition Magazine*, and many others.

Stephanie lives in Brooklyn, NY, with her husband and daughter. In her spare time, she loves traveling, trying new foods, and spending time with friends and family.

Connect with Stephanie online:

Website – NutritionHungry.com

Instagram – @NutritionHungry

Facebook – Facebook.com/NutritionHungry

Printed in the USA
CPSIA information can be obtained
at www.ICGtesting.com
JSHW070731111123
51657JS00008BA/177

9 781646 119097